FINDING YOUR WAY

to say

Goodbye

FINDING YOUR WAY

to say

Goodbye

Comfort for the Dying and Those Who Care for Them

Harold Ivan Smith

ave maria press   Notre Dame, IN

© 2002 by Ave Maria Press, Inc.

www.avemariapress.com

International Standard Book Number: 0-87793-975-6

Cover and text design by Brian C. Conley

Printed and bound in the United States of America.

Library of Congress Cataloging-in-Publication Data
Smith, Harold Ivan, 1947-
    Finding your way to say goodbye : comfort for the dying and those who care
for them / Harold Ivan Smith.
        p. cm.
Includes bibliographical references.
    ISBN 0-87793-975-6 (pbk.)
    1. Terminally ill--Religious life. 2. Death--Religious aspects--Catholic
Church. 3. Terminally ill--Psychology. 4. Death--Psychological aspects. I. Title.
    BX2347.8.S5 .S64 2002
    248.8'6175--dc21
                                                                    2002007242
                                                                    CIP

"If my life ended tomorrow, would I be happy with how I spent today?"
—Nancy Lanoue

Contents

Part One

Introduction

Not everyone gets to know ahead of time what you now know.

Death, for many, is a surprise— a sneaky, stealthy thief
  striking without warning
  like that sad September morning.

Whether heart attack, stroke, vehicular or workplace accident,
  plane crash, earthquake, terrorist attack—
  there are lots of ways to die.
  "He never knew what hit him!" or "She died instantly"
  seems, for many, the best "way to go."

While that means dying without prolonged suffering,
  it means dying without giving and receiving,
  dying without rememberings and reflections,
  dying without exchanged goodbyes,
  and without provisions for the adventure.

YOU now know that you are dying.

Perhaps others know, too. Or soon will know.

It's as if someone has reset your lifeclock.

The language has dramatically shifted from
    "We're all going to die someday" to
    "*I* am going to die." Or "*I* am dying."
    Am becomes one power-packed word
    that wallops like a slap on the face.

You cannot pretend that you do not know now that you know!

YOUR approaching death will sadden loved ones and friends.
    Scare some. Anger some. Confuse some.

Some will not hear you out.
    They will interrupt with appeals to God, to Mary, to the
        doctors
    or plead for trips to famous medical institutions
    or trying alternative treatments.

They will say, "We will fight this." *We?!* . . .
    although they have little understanding.

Some will shush you. Change the subject. Leave the room.
    Trivialize your condition. Dismiss your fears.
    Or go on and on with some story about an individual
    with the same diagnosis who is now running marathons!

"Marathons! You'd never even know he had been sick!
Can you believe it?" Well, can you?

Others will drag in mounds of printouts from the Internet
    including the latest research by "Dr. So-and-So,"
    one of the "star" specialists who can do miracles,
    three hundred sixty-five days a year.
    Or testimonials to some breakthrough drug or therapy.
    "Oh," they will exclaim,
    "You just have to try this! *This* could do the trick!"

Some will suggest that you go on some bizarre diet
    like the "beet" diet (beets three times a day,
    raw beet snack, beetshakes . . .).
    Or fast to purify your system.

Or inventory your self-defeating behaviors that led to this illness.

And there's always some new clinic in Mexico
    or yoga and acupuncture or beet juice enemas,
    magnets or crystals,
    consultations with New Age gurus,
    and other remedies someone claims
    halted death in its tracks.

It doesn't halt death.
    At best, it merely resets the game clock.
    At worst, it. . . .
    No one—no one—gets out of here alive!
    Sooner or later death comes a callin' again.

CONSIDER yourself blessed when individuals come
   not with answers, solutions, suggestions, advice,
   but with a generous portion of themselves.

Consider yourself blessed whenever
   someone listens to you,
   listens intently to sentences that trail off,
   to sentences that ramble,
   to sentences that are punctuated with sobs or silences.

SEEMINGLY, death is the next major event in your life
   and in the lives of your loved ones.

If a miracle is in the wings, now would be a good time!

Admittedly, a loved one could go before you—
   all that stuff about "getting hit by a bus."

You've been tipped off.
   So, what will you do with the warning?

A diagnosis can be turned into good,
   life-changing knowledge.

A diagnosis can be turned into time to listen, time to hear;
   time to finish up, time to resolve;
   time to get around to doing what you haven't gotten
      around to;
   time to ask questions and ponder answers;
   time to wrestle with the mysteries and unexplainables,

time to be strong, time to be weak,
time to confront fears, time to shed tears,
and time to get your affairs in order.

Most importantly it becomes a time to make choices
to die while living. To die well.
To die with few, perhaps no, "if onlys. . . ."

DYING is not a play with all the dialogue and plot
scripted by some unseen playwright. No!
You sit in the director's chair.

Many of your lines in this drama will be spontaneous,
some will surprise you and loved ones.

Some of your best lines—
the ones that will be long remembered and repeated—
will be preceded and followed by silence or by ellipsis
remarks.

It will not be wise for you to put up a "Do NOT disturb!" sign.

You need others. This is a drama, not a one actor show.
Ignore the temptation to be The Loner.

You will not be doing friends a favor
by keeping them from walking with you
on this portion of the shadowed trail.

This is no time for bravado or tough "I can take its!"
    Or to dust off your best imitation of tough guys
    John Wayne, Charles Bronson, or Sylvester Stallone.

If you make the choice to pretend "tough,"
    you exclude loved ones and friends
    and all those who made up the "others" of your life
    from walking beside you on a path, that sooner or later,
    they too must walk.

If you exclude individuals, you keep them
    from witnessing your dying
    and learning from your dying
    and growing from your dying.

You keep them from the lessons that cannot be found
    in a book or homily or lecture or video.

Indeed, some of the knowledge you will need you might have
      known
    if only someone had let you in on her dying.

DYING is about making choices.
    Good choices. Tough choices. Necessary choices.
    Soul-testing and soul-trying choices.

It's a choice to live fully, to live richly
    until death comes.

It's a choice to dare:
"Go ahead, Mr. Death. Take your best shot!"

It's a choice to make room for all the ordinary things
    so often overlooked, ignored, or faintly appreciated:
    sunrises and sunsets, snowfalls and thunderstorms,
    "I shouldn't" second helpings,
    ice cream cones on hot summer days,
    piping hot pizzas on frigid cold nights,
    cookies hot off the pan,
    frolicking dogs, curious cats,
    billowing clouds, ferocious lightning,
    the kiss of a breeze on a cheek,
    the touch of a particular human hand,
    the kindness of clean sheets, fresh gowns that cover the
        backside,
    a real bath or shower, a massage,
    and the children. Oh yes, the children.

WHAT will you miss from life's bountiful buffet
    if you choose to die in isolation,
    snarling, "Go away! Stay away!"?

Dying people learn that great moments happen,
    unlikely but oh-so-holy gifted moments,
    when if you listen closely
    you detect the rustling of angel wings.

NOW that you know, you face choices as you find your way:
    the choice to recognize the loss,
    the choice to react to the loss,

the choice to re-"collect" and re-experience
    the palate of your relationships,
the choice to let go, reluctantly, gradually, deliberately,
the choice to bask in God's outrageous grace,
the choice to tighten fingers around
    God's ancient promise:
    "I will never leave you or forsake you!"
If God ever starts breaking promises
    it won't be with you!

It is a choice to remember that
    the same God who listened to Jesus that awful night
    will listen to you on your awful nights.

The same God who listened to Jesus' plea, "If it is possible . . ."
    will listen to your petitions about possibilities.

The same God who sent angels to strengthen Jesus
    will dispatch angels to your dying place.

IN the days ahead,
    however many or few,
    you can choose well. You can live well.
    You can die well!

You must not be intimidated
    simply because your choices
    make others uncomfortable
    or inconvenience medical personnel.

DYING is about making the choice
    to see today—
    this day's particular preciousness.

And to seize it!
    To leave your fingerprints all over it.
    To squeeze the nectar from the day
        as you would a lemon or an orange.

DYING is about making the choice to confess,
    "This is the day the Lord has made!"
    I may not do much rejoicing
    but I will not squander it!

DYING is not nearly as passive an experience
    as some would have you believe –
    an experience that leaves you whimpering
    in an enforced helplessness,
    "What can I do?"

The question only you can answer:
    "What can I do with *this* minute, *this* hour, *this* day?"

IF you follow the suggestions in this book,
    you are going to be rather busy
    choosing to live well
    now that you know.

Here's the reality:
    In a hundred moments of our lives

we have done something we didn't know we could do
because someone said,
"Here, I'll go first. Just follow me."
It's not just Jesus that goes before us
        but Mary, Tom, Kevin and Irene, and. . . .

Jesus went first.
    He defanged death.
    He gift-wrapped resurrection for you.
    It's easy to talk about resurrection, even debate it,
    but now you get to anticipate it
    and soon experience it.
    To be more alive than you have ever been.

Jesus promised, and promises,
    "I go to prepare a place for you AND
    I will come back and walk with you
    so that, where I am, there you may also be. Always."

It's easy to believe in Easter on Easter.
    It's tougher to believe in Easter at 2 a.m.
        or when you are puked out
        or when pain is pounding
        or when the demons are menacing
        or when friends are cliché-ing!

It's tough to believe Jesus' promise
    when the specialist leaves the room
    after dropping the pronouncement.

It's tough to believe Jesus' promise
    when being wheeled out of a hospital,
    too weak to walk after a chemo treatment.

It's tough to believe Jesus' promise
    waiting to be changed.

It's tough to believe Jesus' promise
    when memories of lovemaking
    mock the body's realities.

It's tough to believe in Jesus when yet another specialist
    suggests yet another procedure that *might* work.

DYING you will experience a lot of tough "to trust in Jesus"
    moments.
But if it's not true today,
    if it's not true in the gut-wrenching,
    heart-stretching moments of dying,
    then it's not true on Easter Day!

But, the good news is, it is true!

YOU think you have been to some parties and "doings" here.
    Just wait. You just wait.
    You will never believe what "party" means
        until you show up for The Party.

Eucharist has been merely the appetizer
    for the great gathering around God's table.

All the suffering will seem insignificant when Jesus exclaims,
"Good to see you. You had it tough.
Let me show you around. I've got some people
I want you to meet."

A WOMAN, now dying, loved chocolate milkshakes.
At 2:00 a.m., a heartbroken friend
wiping away tears, drove until she found an all night diner
and bought a dozen milkshakes. Chocolate, of course.

In the middle of that last night
family, friends, nurses, chaplain gathered for one final toast
and sipped milkshakes as Judy tasted her last sip
then breathed her last.

It was a "Judy" moment. A gift for the memories.
They "made love." Real love.
And, in a way, they all received provisions for their journey
into a land without Judy.

People still talk about milkshakes at 2:00 a.m.!
Or was it eucharist at 2:00 a.m.?

YOU have to find YOUR way in this dying.
But you do not have to figure it out by yourself.
And sometimes, you have to put down the map,
and take a long look out the windshield and say,
"I think it's this way."

Defining a "good and blessed" death

Only one thing is impossible for man— to avoid death.
—Saint Anthony the Great[1]

One Jewish proverb says, "Everyone knows he will die—but no one believes it." Maybe you will die, but not me. Now a moment that began with, "I'm afraid I have some bad news" says, "Yeah, I mean you!" It's the ultimate "Tag—you're it!"

Over the centuries, women and men, well acquainted with death, have wished for a "good" death: in the presence of those they love, in familiar surroundings, and, hopefully, reasonably free from pain. So important was this desire that a whole area of knowledge developed, *ars moriendi*, the art of dying. Sermons, books, tracts, and music offered insights. People kept tinkering with the subject until *ars bene moriendi*—the art of dying *well*—emerged.

What is a "good" death, anyway? Few die a good death. In fact, a high percent die in pain, suffering emotionally, hands restrained, tubes and wires attached everywhere, drugged, and too often in an outrageously loud and bright place.

Although death is as common as birth, and although marketing people have created trendy "birthing suites" to attract customers to hospitals, few hospitals have "dying suites." Dying is a medical issue best left to the professionals. How about a nice room at the end of the hall? Out of sight and out of mind. In many hospitals, death can only be considered a defeat. We "lost" the guy in 404.

The way most of us will die is not particularly "good." Our ancestors would stare in disbelief at our ways of experiencing the inevitable. Our culture is obsessed with improving everything—well, except death. One might ask, what about hospice? Hospice is a wonderful gift to the dying. But unfortunately, few patients get to take full advantage of the gifts of hospice. Why? Because of the presence of medicines, machines, and surgical techniques, whose very existence—and ready access (for a price)—encourage their use and overuse. When we say, "Do everything humanly possible," the efforts often are inhumane. Few doctors recommend hospice for fear that families will think they are "throwing in the towel" medically. Too many physicians consider hospice the last resort, the last straw. Like a college fight song, it's "Fight. Fight! Fight!!!" for physicians.

Kenneth Vaux and Sara Vaux, in *Dying Well*, offer a working definition for a good death. A "good" death is ending one's days

- relieved of disabling pain,
- surrounded by family and friends,

- attended by sensitive caregivers,
- reconciled with all persons,
- in justice and humanity with the world,
- at peace with God.[2]

Take a moment and think about each of these elements. Which sounds right to you? Which do you want? Which are you unwilling to do without?

Relieved of disabling pain. There is no need to end one's life painfully when pain medications are readily available.

Surrounded by family and friends. The Hebrews commonly used the phrase "gathered to his people" to describe dying (Gn 35: 29). But a part of a good death is gathering those individuals we have loved to be "with us" before and as we set off for our ultimate bon voyage.

Attended by sensitive caregivers. Hospitals, nursing homes, and hospices are filled with wonderful caregivers. Be sure you are getting the very best in care. Talk to your family about concerns, and do not be afraid to ask for better, more compassionate care.

Reconciled with all persons. Notice the qualifier in that phrase: reconciled with *all* persons. This is nonnegotiable for a good death. Maybe you've read about Native American tribes who bury the horse with an individual because he will need a good horse in the next world. Will you need resentment in the next world? Then why hang on to it?

What is in your backpack? Unresolved conflicts, resentments—several of which have festered to unbelievable proportions. Few people would fondle a cobra, but they do fondle resentments. You have seen enough television to know that murderers attach rocks to make a body sink to the bottom of a lake. Too many people die with resentments attached to their hearts.

In justice and humanity with the world. You may find it easy to be "in justice" with family and friends, but what about the larger world? My mother, a Southerner, had strong feelings toward African Americans, at times allowing stereotypes to color her world. Amazingly, most of the people who cared for her in the last weeks of her life were people of color. Maybe she will have neighbors in heaven who are persons of color. Perhaps God was just getting her used to the idea so that when she opened the blinds of her condo in heaven she wasn't surprised that her new neighbors were Nigerian.

Clark had this strong homophobia that hurt a lot of people. Yet, he did not know that the male nurse who took such good care of him was gay. (He did not fit any of Clark's stereotypes.) Even when Clark let loose a virulent tirade one day, the male nurse offered grace.

At peace with God. Dying offers you an opportunity to develop an intimacy with God—an offer some have kept at arm's length throughout life. Readers have appreciated Cardinal Bernardin's spiritual classic, *The Gift of Peace,* written as he died of cancer. I have been taken by his vulnerability, "Throughout my spiritual journey I have struggled to become closer to God." He owned his difficulty in "letting go." "By letting go, I mean the ability to release from our grasp those things which inhibit us from developing an intimate relationship with the Lord."[3] For the Cardinal a terminal illness became an extraordinary pilgrimage to God.

One diagnosis teaches us, in Bernardin's words, "how little control we really have and how important it is to trust in him."[4] Little surprise that in those moments when you learned the diagnosis, your first words were, "Oh, God!"

An intimate relationship with the Lord is not just for spiritual giants like Joseph Bernardin. It is for the likes of you and me. Peace is God's gift for all. There are no asterisks, "Well, except for the following. . . ."

God is outrageously gracious. He will turn no one away— even one whose "God have mercy on me!" is a dying gasp or thought. In the words of Charles de Foucauld, "God—who knows what clay He shaped us from and loves us more than a mother can her child—God, who does not lie, has told us that He will not repulse anyone who comes to Him."[5]

One Old Testament passage has been a source of great comfort to me. "He devises ways so that a banished person may not remain estranged from him" (2 Sm 14:14). Megory Anderson, a death midwife, had an incredible experience accompanying eleven-year-old Katy, dying of cancer. Katy struggled with questions that she was hesitant to discuss with her family, so she talked with Anderson. Anderson was stunned by the intensity of Katy's assumption that God was angry at her. "Isn't God going to do something bad to me when I die?" This child had concluded that illness was a one-two punch from God. Adults suffer with the same distortion, but not all get a caring presence in their lives like Megory Anderson.

Anderson reflected a moment. "Katy, who do you love most in the world?"

Without hesitation Katy answered, "My mom. Well, my dad and Phillip [a brother] too, but best of all my mom."

"OK, when you close your eyes and feel how much you love your mom and how much she loves you, it's pretty wonderful, isn't it?" Katy nodded.

"Well, I think if you take that much love and multiply it a hundred times, you still can't come close to how much God loves you."[6]

Those who work with the dying are often on the front row to witness some of the most unbelievable grace dramas. Peter was dying of AIDS complications. The estrangement between his father and himself was loud, cruel, and raw-edged. Over a decade they repeatedly wounded each other. Now, he would bring Peter's mother to the hospital and sit in the lobby waiting. Not once did he go to his son, although Peter repeatedly called out for his father—just as he had as a small boy when nightmares frightened him.

Family members and friends tried to get this macho man to spend some time reconciling with his son. "Hell, no!" he responded in a voice that intimated, "Mind your own damn business!"

The priest who loved both men tried to build a bridge between them but to no avail. Repeatedly, this caring priest called out to God to help him do the impossible before time ran out.

Now, Peter was dying. The family had held vigil for hours, when in walked his father, a huge steelworker, pushing aside family members to get to his son. And the hugest tears some had ever seen dropped from the father's face. He scooped that boy from the bed and rocked him in his arms.

"It is all right, I'm here. Nothing's going to harm you." Few people saw the scene clearly because so many were crying.

God walks into your dying early. He is not sitting in a lobby waiting for the dramatic moment. Listen closely and you will hear, "It is all right, I'm here. Nothing's going to harm you."

Three thousand years ago a psalmist wrote, "The Lord will keep you from all harm—he will watch over your life; the Lord will watch over your coming and going both now and forevermore" (Ps 121:7-8).

The God who has watched over you from your first breath will as zealously watch over you as you draw your last breath and breathe eternity's first breeze.

In all that I have written in sermons, lectures, and workshops, I have never been able to craft a sentence as hope-packed as Donna Schaper's: "God is spreading grace around in the world like a five-year-old spreads peanut butter: thickly, sloppily, eagerly."[7] And God, like a five-year-old, gets it all over everywhere.

The birth canal must be a scary place to a baby. So, the dying canal can be equally scary. But God uses both to bring life. One to bring earthly life—life that will someday end; the other to bring eternal life that will never end.

Virginia Morris, in *Talking About Death Won't Kill You*, summarizes the necessity for dying,

> . . . the plain truth is that aside from suddenly collapsing dead on the eighteenth hole, there is no easy way out of this world. It takes nine months and a lot of hard pushing to get people into it, and it usually takes at least that much effort to get them out.

In her assessment, dying is difficult work because

It involves pain and grief, and it would be pure folly to imagine that it didn't or that we could avoid suffering altogether. When we talk about "dying well" or a "good death," we have to remember that no death is truly "good"; we are always talking about making the best of a difficult, inevitable, and very human event.[8]

Your major task is making the best of this difficult and inevitable human experience. You can make the best of death and let death make the best of you!

A thought for reflection

When you believe in God, death is a doorway,
not a wall. And while I may have cancer,
it doesn't have me.
—Vivian to her sister Patti LaBelle[9]

A prayer

O Mary, mother of Jesus!
You did not abandon Jesus in his suffering.
Be near me as my dying hour approaches.
You will not abandon anyone
who seeks your aid and comfort.
You will not start with me.
Most of the time I believe that.
Help me, Mary,
in the moments when I doubt.

Breath meditation

Breathe in: Holy Mary, be with me now

Breathe out: and in the hours of my dying.

Meditating on the psalms

When you don't know what to say, do, or think, let the psalms speak for you and to you.

The psalms have been a treasured oasis of encouragement, hope, and strength for generations. One third of the psalms are laments which, in my mother's words, "really let God have it!" The psalmists knew that God can handle anger and frustration. Listen to the brutal honesty:

> How long, O Lord? Will you forget me forever?
> How long will you hide your face from me?
> —Psalm 13:1

You can join that long line of dying persons who have clung to the psalms. Think about the individuals across the ages who have recited, "Yea, though I walk through the valley of the shadow of death, I will fear no evil; for thou art with me" (Ps 23:4, KJV). Saint Francis, Thérèse de Lisieux, John XXIII, Mother Teresa, Thomas Merton, Maximilian Kolbe, Joseph Bernardin, all called to God, yet, it does not say "for thou art with the saints." It says *with me*. God hangs out with the likes of us! Especially so, the closer we get to eternity's gate.

Jesus borrowed from the psalmist in voicing his sense of abandonment as he died, "My God, my God, why have you forsaken me?" (Mt 27:46) So, whenever you feel abandoned, quote Jesus, the psalmist, and the saints. If Jesus was not original in crafting his prayer, you don't have to be either. Borrow a psalm phrase and wear it out.

I suggest you audition a psalm fragment at the end of one of the chapters. Try it out a few times. "Test drive" it. Does it have bang for you? Practice with one Jesus used: "My God, my God, why have you forsaken me?"

Pretend you are auditioning for a part in a play; the script includes these lines. Try them in different voices. Do your best imitation of John Wayne, Joan Crawford, Clint Eastwood, or Mr. T.

"My God! My GOD!!! WHY have you forsaken ME?"

(You have permission to get into this. Trust me, God is not going to fling a lightning bolt at you. After all, people who love each other occasionally raise their voices and generously use exclamation marks.) Now try it again.

Not bad. Trying thinking the fragment. Inhale as you think: *"My God, my God . . ."*; exhale as you think: *"why have you forsaken me?"*

Again. (Don't forget the exclamation marks.)

Actually, this prayer stimulates your breathing. Many dying people develop pneumonia or chest congestion because they breathe so shallowly. So, take a big, big breath: *"My God, my God . . ."* and push, push the air out. Push!: *"why have you forsaken me?"*

Repeat the phrases as many times as you can. You will be surprised how calming breathing the psalms can be. Long before modern medicine, the dying relied on the psalms.

Emphasis psalms. Recite this psalm fragment from Psalm 63: "O Lord, you are my God, early will I seek you." Now, close your eyes and slowly repeat: "O Lord, you are my God, earnestly I seek you."

Repeat the psalm phrase ten times, each time emphasizing a different word.

O Lord, you are my God, earnestly I seek you

O **LORD**, you are my God, earnestly I seek you.

O Lord, **YOU** are my God, earnestly I seek you.

What word "leaped out" at you or became alive for you? Try repeating this phrase, deleting a word from the end.

As you breathe you are memorizing scripture which will be useful in moments when you lie awake, afraid or lonely. At the first inkling of despair, begin softly reciting the psalm fragment. Try: *"You will not abandon me to the grave"* (Ps 16:10). Make the phrase stronger, *"God* will not abandon *me* to the grave." Or "God will not abandon [your name] to the grave." Try the fragment as a petition, "God, do not abandon me to the grave."

To use this phrase as a breathing prayer, inhale on: *"You will not abandon me"*; exhale on: *"to the grave."* You will die but you are not being abandoned! What we sing, "May a choir of angels come to meet you . . . may they lead you to paradise . . ." will be reality.

Before beginning a new chapter, spend some time with the breath meditation. Some will mean more to you than others. The more you practice the phrases, the more the fragments will be "cued up" for when the pain medication wears off, when anxiety sets in, when you are vomiting, when you are alone, when you are wondering where the nurse is, as you wait for a procedure. In such moments many find the psalm fragments comforting.

Teach family members or friends to use these psalm phrases. Ask them to join you in breathing psalms on a particularly tough day.

A Jewish farmer, through carelessness, did not get home before the start of sabbath. So, he had to spend the night and the next day in the field. To say the least, the rabbi was angry with him.

"And just what did you do out there all day? Did you pray?"

"Oh, rabbi, I am not good at praying. So, I simply recited the alphabet all day and let God form the words for himself."

The most authentic prayer may be, "Oh, God!"

A thought for reflection

The resurrection is God's way of revealing that nothing
that belongs to God will ever go to waste.
What belongs to God
will never get lost—not even our mortal bodies.
    —Henri Nouwen[10]

An audit

Glance through the breath meditations in this book. Pick out one and make it into a sign for your room or ask someone who is good with graphics to "dress it up" for you.

"God **WILL NOT** abandon **ME** to the grave!"

Visitors, medical personnel, housekeeping staff will notice the sign and be encouraged. The sign could invite the question, "How can you be so hopeful?"

A prayer

God, I cannot see you
    yet you see me.
God, I cannot hear you
    yet you hear me.
God, I cannot cheer me
    yet you can cheer me.
God, I cannot heal me
    yet you can heal me.
Speak to me through the psalms
    as you have spoken to
    so many before me.

Breath meditation

Breathe in: My soul is weary with sorrow;

Breathe out: strengthen me according to your word. (Ps 119:28)

Part Two

Admitting that you know

It's never the same as it was before. Now that you know you are
mortal and your life will be forever changed by that.
—Andre Lorde[11]

One of my parents' favorite television shows in the fifties was
I've Got a Secret. A guest with a "secret" answered questions from a
celebrity panel. Tame television but occasionally quite fascinating.

Unfortunately, many terminal patients act as if they were part
of a big secret. Historian Cornelius Ryan, author of *The Longest
Day*, went to intricate lengths to disguise his illness from his publishers, fearful of reaction by critics and readers that would affect
his last book's acceptance and impact sales that would provide for
his family's future. Ryan had a secret.

Admittedly, you are fortunate that you know that the prognosis is terminal or life-threatening. *Fortunate?* Yes, because some families collude to keep critical information from the dying individual.

Or they hide information from certain family members. Or they will not discuss the end-of-life issues, funeral plans, etc. Some individuals delay medical treatment until the disease is rampant.

My friend Father Joe Nassal tells a story about an elderly nun who was dying but who chose to be positive about the diagnosis. Somehow, she stumbled onto her medical records and read this assessment, "Sister is in denial." Sister was not in denial; rather, from the first, she took this piece of data and blended it into the batter of her life. The diagnosis was one factor—not the factor governing her life.

Len Butler described his experience taking radiation treatments at Mayo Clinic during the Christmas holidays. The doctor could not believe that Len was staying in Rochester rather than going home. Finally the doctor blurted out, "Man, don't you realize this is your *last* Christmas!"

Len responded, "Maybe it is but maybe it isn't!" He determined to live long enough to send the "predicting" doctor several Christmas cards. Len immediately began planning his first annual "last" Christmas. In a support group a man comforted Len, "Oh, that's just doctor talk. I've had four 'last' Christmases so far."[12]

It's not the diagnosis. It is what you *do* with the diagnosis!

The mortality rate is one out of one! No one gets out of here alive. Yet, there is this cultural collusion to pretend someone is going to beat the system. "And, it might as well be me." Denying the truth limits choices.

Own the truth. By doing so, you give others the courage to own their truth. Admit that you know, but don't make that the end.

A thought for reflection

Sooner or later every one of us becomes an expert on loss.

—David Wolpe, *Making Loss Matter*[13]

An audit

Name four ways you have admitted your diagnosis.

I have _____

I have _____

I have _____

I have _____

A prayer

God, Comforter,

though a citizen of the valley of the shadow of death

I will not fear when I sense you near.

Breath meditation

Breathe in: O God, you are my God,

Breathe out: earnestly I seek you. (Ps 63:1)

Releasing control

It is not so much what happens to you. It is how you choose to respond.

There are three great realities in life. The things I can do *something* about, the things I can do *little* about, and the things I can do *nothing* about. Wise is the person who knows the subtleties between categories.

Jimmy Carter was defeated by Ronald Reagan in 1980. Yet, life for Carter was not over. He reminisces,

> Although my disappointment was great, I kept it bottled up for a long time. Slowly, it began to ease as new challenges presented themselves that needed to be met. Right after the defeat, I tried to think of everything we could possibly accomplish

during the few months left in the White House, and arranged the list according to feasibility, setting an ambitious schedule for myself and for those around me.[14]

There is wisdom in Carter's response. While others would have been paralyzed by the defeat, he became motivated. I am amazed by patients who receive the terminal diagnosis, nurse their initial emotions, then live with a new deliberation and intensity.

Effective coaches keep one eye on the game clock but the other eye on the playing field. So can you.

A thought for reflection

A saint was once asked, while playing happily with his companions, what he would do if an angel told him that in a quarter of an hour he would die and have to appear before the judgment seat of God. The saint promptly replied that he would continue playing because he is certain these games are pleasing to God.

—St. John Bosco[15]

An audit

In the time you have left, what are the most important things for you to do, complete, or accomplish?

I want to _____

I want to _____

I want to _____

I want to _____

I want to _____

I want to _____

A prayer
God, what do I do with "today"?
How can I live with intensity today?
Any ideas?
I am open to your suggestions.

Breath meditation
Breathe in: May the words of my mouth . . .

Breathe out: be pleasing in your sight. (Ps 19:14)

Asking your questions

There is no such thing as a bad question. The issue is not with the questions, or even how we ask them. The issue is where we go with questions. Any question that brings us to God for an answer is a good question.
—Dave Dravecky[16]

On Thursday mornings at the Kentucky School of Mortuary Science, our dean, a most intense man, would walk into class and demand, "What questions do you wish to ask?" (We quickly learned to take him up on his "invitation" because his alternative was pop quizzes that no one could pass!)

So I ask you, "What questions do you wish to ask?" Many people will want you to avoid asking questions, especially the hard questions. "Oh, it's not for us to ask the reasons why," they will interrupt. "God knows what he is doing." Easy for them to say!

Questions come in two waves: initial and long-term. Or perhaps I could say, low yield and high yield.

You may have already asked what many assume is the biggie: "How long do I have?" And you may have a "working" answer. But the big question is: what will I do with the time I have left?

Other initial questions are:

1. Why?
2. Why me?
3. Why now?
4. What have I done to deserve this?
5. Why am I being punished?

You may have some tentative answers. There is nothing wrong with the questions or with questioning. The issue is to whom do you look for answers, and how much credence do you put in their answers? You need someone to give you permission to ask your questions—especially those that taunt in the night.

Jesus offers you permission. As we saw earlier, it is often helpful to ponder his words from the cross, "My God, my God, why have you forsaken me?" (Mt 27:46). That may be the greatest string of words ever preceding a question mark! Other words, even in the best Lenten homilies, have sounded too wimpy.

While I believe scripture accurately captures Jesus' experience, I wonder about the accuracy of the punctuation. I think the words reverberated like thunder between earth and heaven that Good Friday. I suggest this to be more accurate punctuation:

"My God! My God!!! Why! have you forsaken me?!!!!"

Perhaps you have already tried out the question a few times. You may feel guilty—or someone is making you feel guilty—for daring to voice such thoughts. You have a right to ask your "why" questions.

Sometimes, the only way we can ask the question is with an exclamation mark (or two or three) following the question mark. I think exclamation marks fell from Jesus' mouth as surely as tears streamed from his eyes and sweat from his forehead.

You may not be asking "why" questions aloud, but you may be rehearsing them deep in the corridors of your mind. Keep asking.

You may not be asking "why" questions, but family members and friends are. By this point you may be able to sense the unanswered questions on the minds of family members or friends. Give them permission to verbalize their questions.

Beware of the censor who tries to talk you out of your questions. Beware of one who interrupts when your question threatens the safety of his or her answers. Beware of anyone who suggests that questioners take their questions to the hallway, waiting room, or coffee shop.

If Jesus can ask why, so can you!

Jesus' "why?" is permission for you to let your questions loose.

In the hours that have more than sixty minutes—often between midnight and sunup—"why" questions blow across your mind and heart like tumbleweeds blowing across the prairie. You may feel like TV's Detective Colombo, searching for some missing clue that will lead to the "Ah HA!" moment that will, at last, provide the missing piece to the puzzle: "That's it! Now I know why I am dying."

Frederica Mathewes-Green offers an alternative.

> The only useful question in such a time is not "Why?" but "What's next?" What should I do next? What should be my response to this ugly event?

How can I bring the best out of it? How can God
bring Resurrection out of it?"[17]

Ask your questions.

A thought for reflection

. . . have patience with everything unresolved in your heart
and try to love the questions themselves as if they were locked
rooms or books written in a very foreign language. Don't search
for the answers, which could not be given you now, because you
would not be able to live them. And the point is, to live everything. Live the questions now. Perhaps then, someday far in the
future, you will gradually, without ever noticing it, live your way
into the answer. . . .
—Rainer Maria Rilke[18]

A prayer

God, I can live with this disease but
I cannot live without
some hint of an explanation.
I have two haunting questions,
Why?!!!
Can you help me?!!!

Breath meditation

Breathe in: Do not be far from me

Breathe out: for trouble is near. (Ps 22:11)

Dealing with privacy

I was anxious to get home, but sensitive about how I would appear
to my children, hobbling around with the Foley catheter. . . .
I didn't quite know how to explain this to my children, but three-
year-old Alexander obviously got it because he told his classmates
that "Daddy went on a trip and bought a tee-tee bag."
—Hamilton Jordan[19]

Hospital gowns may be the least of your privacy anxieties. A portable potty in the corner of an elegant bedroom, although convenient, will seldom add to the ambiance of the room. (Maybe someday Martha Stewart will offer suggestions on decorating portable potties.)

For some, it is not the dying that is so difficult, but the systematic stripping of our bodyhood. Many die angry that their bodies have so betrayed them. For those who have worked hard to define and maintain "body image," the loss can be devastating.

Privacy issues are significant. Some decide that they do not want friends to see them as they are now. "I want them to remember me as I *was*. . . ." Many will not visit saying, "I wanted to respect their privacy" or "I don't know what to say." For those who do not know what to say, "You look like hell" can jumpstart some fascinating conversations.

Hospitals, nursing homes, and hospices ask individuals to surrender their privacy in order to facilitate care. Many people die with a continuous parade of "stranger" caregivers. Privacy may be further challenged if you are being treated in a teaching hospital because students are often shuffled in and out of your room. If you have a private room during your hospitalizations, consider yourself blessed.

Talk with your caregivers about your need for privacy. Tell them your desires, and trust that they will try their best to honor your requests. Find a place (as best as you can) that is your very own, a place for you to be alone even in the midst of the busyness of the hospital or nursing home.

A thought for reflection

I want to stand in your sight
own what I am
and be free of all human opinion and judgment.
I am what I am—
one loved lavishly by God in a life history.
—John Eagan[20]

A prayer

God, take my frustrations over my loss of privacy
and bombard them with your grace.
Take this illness and fill it with your grace.
Take my despair and diffuse it with your grace.
Take my anxiety and replace it with your grace.

Breath meditation

Breathe in: According to your love remember me,

Breathe out: for you are good, O Lord. (Ps 25:7)

Grasping the present tense

Every once in a while at an airport or a restaurant, someone will come over and ask, "Didn't you used to be Hamilton Jordan?"
—Hamilton Jordan[21]

Until your diagnosis, you, like most American adults, were living in frantic tense—somewhere between present and future tense. Ask me how I am doing and I will tell you how busy I am.

Illness has a way of making shambles of the schedules, calendars, priorities, and responsibilities that compose our lives. All of us live with a promised "some day" when "the rat race" will be won and we can enjoy the good life. Now, this diagnosis casts a pall over the immediate and distant future. All of our hard work and sacrifice is reduced to now tense.

We have a who-knows-how-long now.

Immediately after diagnosis, some will summarize your life in the past tense. "He *used* to be so strong. She *used* to be so bubbly. He *used* to _____" (fill in the blank). *Used* is one of the ugliest four letter words in the English language.

In fact, if you are hospitalized, you can expect someone to walk into your room—even medical personnel—and ask others, "How's *he* doing today?" However sick you are, you may want to rise up and bark, "For your information, 'He is still here. Ask *me* if you want to know how 'he' is doing today!"

Here's the big question: "Who am I *now*?"

You can expect to experience sorrow over your lost future. Not seeing a child, grandchild, great-grandchild born, graduate, or marry. Not experiencing the "golden years" in AARP land. Not reaping the rewards for the years of work and sacrifice.

Okay, maybe your future is not what it once was. But what are you going to do with this precious commodity called today?

Many individuals living with a terminal diagnosis focus on one goal: Making the most of *this* day in order to honor their unique "me."

A thought for reflection

Each death is as individual as the person to whom it happens. None is simple. Each is a reflection of the patient, the life he has lived, the people he has loved, the illness he has endured, and the capacity of those around him to accept the reality of death and to do what needs to be done.

—Virginia Morris[22]

An audit

So, who are you? If I demand in ten minutes to know who you are, how would you complete these statements? (For example, I am male, Caucasian, educated . . . .)

I am _____   I am _____
I am _____   I am _____
I am _____   I am _____
I am _____   I am _____
I am _____   I am _____
I am _____   I am _____

How can you honor who you are, even in the midst of your diagnosis?

A prayer

Jesus, this day is all I have.
Tomorrow is only a faint promise.
Help me be a good steward of these hours
that make up my today.
Give me strength sufficient to meet
the demands of this day.

Breath meditation

Breathe in: He leads me beside quiet waters,

Breathe out: he restores my soul. (Ps 23:2b-3)

*Try this in future tense: "He *will lead* me beside quiet waters, he *will restore* my soul."

Crying

What soap is for the body, tears are for the soul.
—Jewish proverb[23]

I let the tears flow until they dry up. And then I start to think about what I'm crying about. I'm crying about my own death, my departure from people I love, the sense of unfinished business and of leaving this beautiful world. Crying has helped me gradually come to accept the end—the fact that all living things die.
—Morrie Schwartz[24]

"Don't let 'em see you cry" is common but ineffective advice to the dying, as is "Be strong!" and "You've got to fight this with every ounce of your energy!" To males those admonitions sound like, "Take it like a man!"

Remember that big hit from the Sixties, "Now it's Judy's turn to cry. . . ." Try singing, "Now it's [your name] turn to cry. . . ."

Sooner or later, all of us get our time to cry.

"All I do is cry," reports one recently diagnosed individual. Sometimes a well-intentioned person inhibits tears with a simple injunction, "Be strong." Even when there is no exclamation mark, you hear a string of exclamation marks, "Be strong!!!!!"

Make time for tears. You may have the idea that you are to be brave, courageous, put up a front. So you invest a lot of energy trying *not* to cry. It is easier to cry and get it out of the way.

For some males crying is the big no-no! A visible proof of weakness. The slur "Crybaby!" ricochets along the corridors of some masculine hearts.

A girl, age four, was dying with leukemia. Her take-charge mother, anxious to keep the room "positive," decreed that no one could cry in front of the child. Anyone who started to cry was asked to leave. More than once the child's father, feeling tears coming, mumbled something about "having to go to the bathroom" and left. The mother wondered if her daughter died thinking her father had the "weakest bladder in the world."

The child was Robin Bush, daughter of George and Barbara Bush. While Mrs. Bush now regrets her "no tears" policy that fall of 1953, the prohibition made sense at the time.[25]

If you adopt a "No Tears!" policy for yourself, that is your choice. However, do not limit the options of others. Marion, a participant in one of my grief groups, made a pact with the devil, in essence, when she agreed to her dying son's request that there be no tears in front of him. Numerous conversations ended abruptly as Marion dashed for the hall. She kept her promise—but at a cost.

Tears can be a jumpstart for verbalizing a sense of powerlessness and frustration. Allow yourself to be moved by the tears of others for you. Truth be told, most of us feel better after a good cry.

In *Tuesdays with Morrie*, Mitch Albom chronicles Morrie Schwartz's tenderizing due to terminal illness. One Tuesday while talking with Morrie about keeping up with the news in the world, as Morrie described the impact of watching the coverage of the carnage in Bosnia, his eyes "got moist." Mitch, a dutiful American male, tried to change the subject. Morrie, recognizing his protege's discomfort, prodded, "This is okay with you, isn't it? Men crying?"

Albom responded, "Yes," too quickly. Morrie challenged his student.

"Ah, Mitch, I'm going to loosen you up. One day, I'm going to show you it's okay to cry."[26] You may have the same opportunity with your "Mitches." One of your gifts could be giving permission to cry.

As Monsignor Kenneth Velo was flying home to Chicago with his gravely ill friend, Cardinal Bernardin, after an audience with The Holy Father, Bernardin handed him an outline of his funeral plans. Velo began crying. Bernardin did not try to stifle the moment but responded in a lovingly kind voice, "Don't worry. I have cried, too."[27]

Give permission to cry—to yourself, to others. Like milk, "it does a body good."

A thought for reflection

Some sentences can only be
correctly punctuated with tears.

A prayer

God, do my tears
make you as uncomfortable
as they make everyone else?
Sometimes, the tears just ambush me.
I have no idea they are there
waiting for a moment to escape.
Remind me of Mary's tears.
Remind me of Jesus' tears.

Breath meditation

Breathe in: For in the day of trouble

Breathe out: he will keep me safe. (Ps 27:5)

Saying "no" or "NO!" to heroic measures

If you are going to go to all the trouble to die, at least, die well!
—Parker Palmer[28]

Do you want to die with plastic tubes in every orifice of your body? Do you want "plastic" in all the last visual memories of you your family will have? If not, say so now. And say so clearly. Resolutely. Repeatedly.

You will need to anticipate which ones of those who love you will create a ruckus and frighten a physician into ignoring your wishes. Three words in a hospital corridor have the impact of lightning and thunder: *my lawyer* and *lawsuit*. Even the guy that graduated number one at Harvard, Stanford, or Vanderbilt medical school will feel a zing in his colon hearing those terms.

Matta Kelly "cares" about people as a case worker at the University of Illinois Community Outreach Intervention Project. Repeatedly patients plead, "Matta, please, *please* make sure that I am not hooked up to machines."[29] She tells a troubling story about Norma Sanders' death.

Norma had verbalized her wishes: no machines!

Norma had filled out all the forms: no machines!

Repeatedly Norma sought reassurance, "Do you still have my papers, my living will?" Basically she was restating her wishes. "I want to make sure that you take care of me. . . . I don't want to be hooked up to machines."

Do you have any doubts of Norma Sanders' wishes? Yet, in some medical settings, it doesn't matter how many times you have said it, or to whom you have said it. Even if you have "*No machines!*" tattooed on your chest, there is a good probability you will end up hooked up to machines—at least for a while.

When Matta was notified that Norma Sanders was in the hospital, she dashed to the hospital and found Norma "hooked up with tubes and all swollen." For over a month "they were trying this, and trying some other things too."[30] That's the clincher: "*some other things too.*"

Make your wishes known on heroic measures!

A thought for reflection

When we take a terminally ill patient off life support, we are not "pulling the plug," we are "freeing" the patient to die. We are "releasing" her from excessive technology and invasive treatments.

—Virginia Morris[31]

An audit

Take a few moments and think about *your* wishes on heroic measures. How can you communicate your wishes so that everyone understands?

A prayer

God, I want my dying to be as normal as possible.
I do not want to be held captive by some machine.
Give me courage to make my wishes clearly known.
Take me into eternal life on your timing.

Breath meditation

Breathe in: The Lord is my light and my salvation—

Breathe out: whom shall I fear? (Ps 27:1)

Partnering with physicians

Often physicians, families, the whole society is caught up in a myth that we can cure, solve, control any problem that comes along—even death. Many physicians say they practice this way because of pressure from families or fear of litigation.
—Linda Johnson[32]

One of the biggest temptations you may face is to be a "good," compliant, go-along-with-the-doctor patient. "Yes, Doctor. Whatever you say, Doctor." Robert Young won a place in American hearts with his depiction of good ol' Bob Anderson in *Father Knows Best*. Too many today think, "*Doctor* Knows Best."

You and your physician(s) should be a team. However, with some physicians, there can only be one in charge (and often, that's not you). There may come a time when you need to ask, "Who's in this bed? Whose name is on the chart? Me!"

Hamilton Jordan, who has battled three cancers, reminds us that "doctors are only human, and very few have the 'total package' of great skills, extensive experience, up-to-date knowledge of the latest treatments, a wonderful bedside manner, and plenty of time to console you and your family."[33]

Jordan concludes, "the better the doctor, the more likely that he or she will not have everything you want and need." Jordan decided, after weighing the options, "I wanted a doctor whom I could trust and one who thought he could cure me of my disease . . . regardless of the statistics."[34]

What kind of doctor do you want?

Virginia Morris argues, "Doctors arrive at a bedside with their own fears of death, unresolved grief, and uncertainty about how to respond to someone else's loss. . . . They are uncomfortable with death just like the rest of us are."[35]

If your doctor has a fear of death, you may experience some delaying tactics. While your doctor tries something else, the angels on your official welcoming party, with banners and the band and all the hoopla for your grand entrance, sit around the pearly gates waiting like stranded travelers in airport lounges. The angels thought you were dying on Tuesday afternoon. Now it is Thursday morning and they are still waiting.

Technology is one reason people do not visit the dying. The machines and noises and bells and whistles turn dying into something out of a science fiction movie. Our technology is so far ahead of our humanity that many who use or rely on the technology get lost in the process. Agreeing to one procedure may put you on the slippery slope into maximum technology. As you read this, some bright engineers and physicians are devising some new gadget of technology or technique to keep death at bay for a few more days. Just as in medieval times knights marveled with great anticipation watching their newest sword being crafted, "Ah, this is the ultimate!" so do scientists today.

I believe people died better in the days when a family doctor—who knew what the inside of your house looked like and smelled like—attended the dying. The doctor could be summoned in the middle of the night. We were better off when doctors spent time talking to and listening to patients rather than filling out insurance forms or jousting with insurance bureaucrats over coverage limitations or racing on to see the next patient. Given the restraints of managed health care, physicians do not have time to "be" with you, to hear your lament, or to receive your fears.

In the old days B.M.C. (before managed care), your doctor would "be there" to pronounce you dead. Your doctor would "be there" for your family. Your doctor would show up at your funeral mass and be comforted by the same bread and wine your immediate survivors tasted. Your doctor would be available in the weeks, months, years ahead monitoring the bereavement of your survivors.

Few of our modern measures, strategies, drugs, or machines will change the diagnosis if you are dying; in fact, some procedures prolong suffering and heighten spiritual agony and emotional pain.

Moreover the technology isn't free. Jim is not only grieving for his wife but also for the end of life as he knows it. Ten days after she died, he received a hospital bill for almost one-half million dollars. Fortunately Jim has insurance; unfortunately, he pays the first twenty percent. So, he owes $100,000. These nights Jim lies in bed thinking not only about how much he misses his wife, but about paying the hospital bill! And God only knows what bills tomorrow's mail will bring. In the past she always challenged his worrying about money, "Oh, honey, we'll make it through this, somehow. . . ." Jim misses her confident "somehows."

Do you want to die leaving survivors lying in the darkness thinking about where they can come up with the co-pay?

Do you want to be brought back to life, again and again?

Do you want your loved ones to be on an emotional roller coaster?

I have some money saved. I do not want my little stash to go to any hospital to keep me alive when it could honor my will: making educational opportunities for poor students. God will have to physically restrain me in heaven if I realize that money went for technological wizardry when it wasn't necessary or wanted! I am all for research but not on my nearly dead body or on your nearly dead body unless you or I fully understand the implications.

I can say it here, but it is tougher to say to those who will be making my medical decisions. Read my lips: "If I am dying: No machines! *NO machines!*" Even dying, I want to be a good steward of what God has helped me accumulate.

You may not be there yet. You may say, "let's give it a shot. What have we got to lose?" (Answer: Plenty!) Then sign your name on the paperwork and let the accountants start calculating the costs.

One of the greatest gifts you can leave your loved ones is clearly articulated wishes for end-of-life decisions.

Make sure your decision makers know that some physicians may try to charm, con, coerce, guilt your loved ones into abandoning your wishes. Your loved ones are going to be emotionally, spiritually, and physically drained. What may sound like hope to loved ones huddled in a conference room may be about the same as the odds of hitting it big in Vegas!

Admittedly we come into this world attached to an umbilical cord, but is it necessary to be attached to so many plastic umbilical cords when we leave? If you think so, by all means, dance with technology. But if you don't want it "all," if you are ready for God's great adventure called eternity, say so now!

The only way the technology stopped for Norma Sanders was that she had a heart attack and died. I bet she died ticked off that her wishes had been ignored!

A thought for reflection

You do not want to be the patient that your doctor[s] "go to school" on.

—Hamilton Jordan[36]

An audit

Rate on a 1 to 10 scale your confidence in your physician(s):

____ has great skills

____ has extensive experience with my illness

____ has up-to-date knowledge of the latest treatment

____ has a wonderful bedside/deskside manner

____ has time to listen to the end of my sentences

____ has a sense of humor

____ will honor my wishes

Which of these skills is nonnegotiable as far as you are concerned?

A prayer

God, bless my physician(s) [Names].

God, bless my nurse(s) [Names].

God, bless my priest [Name].

Give each insight into how best to treat me.

Give them strength sufficient for the details of my illness.

Give me wisdom in knowing how to interact with these helpers.

Breath meditation

Breathe in: I am still confident of this:

Breathe out: I will see the goodness of the Lord. (Ps 27:13)

Putting choices into writing

It is important to speak to your family, friends, and doctors about your wishes, to let others know exactly what you want to happen when you are no longer able to make that choice. . . .
    —David Kessler[37]

Dying requires lots of choices. It is important that you make your choices clearly known. In most medical facilities there will be one question: *Is that in writing?*

Because we are reluctant to "talk" about death, many people, perhaps most, do not make their wishes clearly and widely known. They hint but never come right out and say: "This is what I want and this is what I do *not* want!"

Words written on paper are like money in escrow. Putting your wishes into writing is a gift to your family. Too many families get "ambushed" in hospital corridors and family lounges because the patient did not clearly verbalize wishes and did not dialogue with loved ones about those wishes. As a result, some family members spend years second-guessing "spur of the moment" decisions. Your family is going to have enough to deal with—without having to wrestle with "Now what do we do?" decisions.

Secondly, make sure your family "hears out" your wishes—especially if tension exists between family members. Do all of your children get along with your spouse? Never underestimate the power of what some call the "Uncle Joe from Saint Louis Syndrome." A family member who has not been involved in your life shows up and demands, "I want . . ."What is the likelihood that your siblings will challenge a spouse/partner's commitment to follow your wishes? If a spouse/partner chooses not to follow your wishes? Will children from a previous marriage(s) be the challengers in what could evolve into the Family Feud Royale?

There are ways to put wishes into writing.

Advance Directives. Here is a sample of one state's wording. (Check with an attorney for your state's guidelines.)

> *I do not want efforts made to prolong my life and I do not want life-sustaining treatment to be provided or continued: 1) If I am in an irreversible coma or persistent vegetative state: or 2) If I am terminally ill and the application of life-sustaining procedures would only serve to delay the moment of my death: or 3) Under any other circumstances where the burdens of the treatment outweigh the expected benefits. I want my agent to consider the relief of suffering and the quality as well as the extent of the possible extension of my life in making decisions concerning life-sustaining treatment.*

Or

I want efforts made to prolong my life and I want life-sustaining treatment to be provided unless I am in a coma or persistent vegetative state which my doctor reasonably believes to be irreversible. Once my doctor has concluded that I will remain unconscious for the rest of my life, I do not want life-sustaining treatment to be provided or continued.

Or

I want efforts made to prolong my life and I want life-sustaining treatment to be provided even if I am in an irreversible coma or persistent vegetative state.

Once your wishes are in writing, there are ways to make it more likely that your choices will be honored.

1. Make sure your proxy, agents, or Durable Power of Attorney for Health Care has a copy. (Remember most Durable Powers of Attorney cover property and finances—but may not allow the proxy to make health care decisions.)

2. Give a copy to your physician for your medical records. Talk it over with your physician so that he or she recalls the conversation and notes the conversation in your medical records. Suppose he or she doesn't note it. What happens if that physician is not present—or available—when decisions need to be made? In some hospitals this guideline rules: "If it isn't written, it (the conversation) didn't happen!" "It will be too late when you are in a coma, at which point *any* relative may insist that you be

kept alive, and the doctors will have to keep the machines on. Afraid of being sued, the doctors will err on the side of doing too much rather than too little."[38]

3. Make sure a copy goes with your charts to the hospital *every time*—especially in the middle of the night or on trips to an emergency room.

4. Make sure your family members know where they can quickly locate the document or provide them with copies of your wishes. Carry copies of Advance Directives in your car or in luggage on extended trips.

5. Talk to your family about your wishes in this document. Create a Committee on My Wishes made up of individuals who can clearly identify your wishes.

6. Show family and friends the documents.

7. Verbalize your wishes. The issue will not be the documents but the clarity of your intentions.

8. Allow questions and concerns to be raised while you are available to answer them.

9. Ask for a verbal pledge of compliance. "You know what I want. Will you insist that these wishes be followed?"

Not unlike in the B-Westerns when the sheriff deputized citizens to help, enlist these individuals to fight *for* the honoring of your wishes. Kessler, after witnessing hundreds of deaths, bemoans the reality, "The dying are not always able to ensure that their dignity will be respected."[39] Dignity is not just about having your bottom covered. Dignity is having your wishes honored.

I witnessed Jack's stated wishes against any heroic measures, just before he went into surgery. Those wishes, however, were ignored until Margaret, his wife, responded to a determined specialist, "I will sue you for everything you have!" Jack's wishes were finally, reluctantly, honored.

10. Number each copy of your Advance Directives and keep track of who you give the copies of your Advance Directives to in case you wish to rescind or change the document.

Debate, discuss, dialogue *now*.

A thought for reflection

Please tell your readers NEVER to trust someone else to carry out their wishes without specifying those wishes in black and white.

—Been There in Chicago[40]

A prayer

Give courage, Lord,
for this uncharted journey,
peacefulness at parting
from all that must be left behind,
and an inner vision of invitation
for all that is better that awaits.
    —*Celtic Daily Prayer*[41]

Breath meditation

Breathe in: The troubles of my heart have multiplied;

Breathe out: free me from my anguish. (Ps 25:17)

Living until dying

The reports of my death are greatly exaggerated.

—Mark Twain[42]

Dying is an invitation to live all our days. Dying is an invitation to make *carpe diem* not just a T-shirt slogan but a lived reality. Dying offers a chance to seize the day and to recognize the particular preciousness of a given day. Dying is a day to day, sometimes hour to hour, learning lab.

The theme running through the memorial service for Mark Bingham, one of the passengers who fought terrorists for control of United Airlines Flight 93, was, "He was the kind of guy who drank life with both hands on the cup."[43] Bingham lived his life even to his dying moments as the plane pummeled into the Pennsylvania countryside.

You can die living!!!

You, too, can live with "both hands on the cup."

"When I go, I want to go. . . ." At one time or another, you have completed that sentence, perhaps joked about it. But now that you have a terminal diagnosis, how are you completing the sentence? Are both of your hands on the cup?

Perhaps, using a boxing analogy, dying is a fifteen-rounder. You can moan in the corner after the third round, "Please, don't ring that bell again." Or you can bolt out of the corner, on your feet, dancing and jabbing, prancing and throwing a full bevy of punches. Remember that Timex line, "It takes a lickin' and keeps on tickin'!" That can be said of you, as well.

You are fortunate to get time to ponder this question: What is it that I must *yet* do to die believing my life has been worth living?

The Prayer after Anointing, "When she is afraid, give her courage . . ."[44] is not limited to dying, but applies in those moments when you are searching for the courage to live until you die. You, although dying, can live well. If you live every one of your days, those who witness your courage will be less afraid of their inevitable summons to live last days.

Live *all* of your days. Let your life, in the words of the Maxwell House coffee claim, "be good to the last" *breath*.

The psalmist wrote, "All the days ordained for me were written in your book before one of them came to be" (139:16). Yes, but exactly how many days do I have left? Life is a game we must play without knowing the exact time remaining on the scoreboard or when the buzzer will sound: game over!

This diagnosis can be a gift: the equivalent of the two-minute warning in professional football.

A thought for reflection

I think death's going to happen to me. It happens at the rate of one per person. There's no way out of it. I'm sometimes tempted when I see someone jogging in the park to yell at 'em, "You're gonna die anyhow."

—Quinn Brisben[45]

An audit

Someone in a grief group quoted a question that I have been unable to forget, "If you knew death was coming within twenty-four hours, what would you have the courage to do that you had not done?" Take some time to "hang out" with that question. Write down all the things you want to do before you die. Then trace your right hand on the list. Offer your list as an offering to God.

Before I die I would like to _____ _____

Before I die I would like to _____

Before I die I would like to _____

Before I die I would like to _____

Before I die I would like to _____

Before I die I would like to _____

A prayer

God, Timekeeper, only you know my number of days
    but you know my longing for more days,
    and for a miracle.
Teach me to number my days wisely.

May my use of all these days
   be pleasing and acceptable in your sight.

Breath meditation

Breathe in: Teach me to number my days aright,

Breathe out: that I may gain a heart of wisdom.
                   (Ps 90:12)

Dealing with the physical changes

Only four more weeks and I'll get my life back. But one does not look forward to a summer on the Vineyard with a bad wig.
—Jackie Onassis[46]

You are living *and* dying in a culture obsessed with the physical body. Ever stood in a funeral home and heard this observation about a corpse, "He sure looks good, doesn't he?"

Martin was "model" handsome; heads turned when he walked into a room. Yet, that physical beauty was stripped from him incrementally by the vindictive appetites of his disease. Tragically, some individuals choose to take their lives before experiencing some of the physical changes. Or they live out their lives in isolation, mimicking Greta Garbo, "I want to be alone."

The dying experience loss of weight, loss of strength, loss of hair, loss of sexual attractiveness, the latter more crucial than most healthy individuals imagine.

The observations, "She looks like death warmed over . . ." or "death on two feet" are hardly helpful. In fact, although we bemoan traditions like Eskimos abandoning their dying and aged on ice floats, we emotionally abandon, too.

If you do not want visitors, are you open to phone calls? Are you open to receiving cards and letters? Are you open to cyber correspondence? Would you like clippings from magazines or newspapers that will amuse or be of interest?

Let people find ways to say that they still think of you as beautiful.

A thought for reflection

How can we honor the physical body, which has been the host of the person for a lifetime, and yet at the same time prepare to discard it?

—Megory Anderson[47]

An audit

Body deterioration is not new. Reflect on this lament from three millennia ago:

My breath is offensive to my wife;
I am loathsome to my own brothers.
Even the little boys scorn me;
when I appear, they ridicule me.
All my intimate friends detest me;
those I love have turned against me.

I am nothing but skin and bones;
I have escaped with only the skin of my teeth.
      —Job 19:17-20

Using this fragment as a guide, create your lament:

_____

_____

_____

_____

_____

Now decide how to live so that the physical changes do not define you.

A prayer

God, I groan when I look in the mirror.
I see revulsion in the eyes of my family.
I sense it in the hesitant touch of friends.
My body is betraying me.
Remind me that you do not turn your eyes
    from what is left of me.
Remind me that you see what-will-be
    when I only see what-once-was.

Breath meditation:

Breathe in: Hear my voice when I call,

Breathe out: be merciful and answer me. (Ps 27:7)

Embracing God

Define yourself radically as one beloved by God: God's love for you and his choice of you constitute your worth and let it become the most important thing in your life.
—John Eagan[48]

Dying has a way of stripping from us all our crutches that offer some sense of comfort or confidence. When it's barium enema time, it doesn't matter if you drove a Lexus to outpatient care or rode the city bus.

If you have defined your value on the trinkets of a consumer economy, or physical attractiveness, that won't bring you much comfort now.

But the good news is this: God longs to be close to you as death wrestles everything you have valued from your grasp. In those moments God offers his loving embrace. God hears your laments.

If it concerns you, it concerns God.

A thought for reflection

The Cry to God as "Father" in the New Testament is not
a calm acknowledgment of a universal truth
about God's abstract fatherhood.
It is the Child's cry out of a nightmare.
—Rowan Williams[49]

A prayer

God,
Sister always said, "All things are possible with God."
I've never been too interested in spiritual things. Until now.
I've been rather confident in my ability to take care of me.
I am reluctant to ask for favors but now. . . .
Help me to feel you in the thick darkness that surrounds me.

Breath meditation

Breathe in: Praise be to God

Breathe out: who has not . . . withheld his love from
                     me. (Ps 66:20)

Expressing anger

God is the only one prepared to handle all your anger at him. If you are ticked off at the Almighty, for his sake (and yours) tell him!
—*John Hewett[50]*

Out of a doctoral seminar with Reginald Johnson one eight-word sentence has never ceased ricocheting off the walls of my heart: "God never chides his children for being children."

If the Bible ever needs to be lengthened by one verse, I would nominate those words. God NEVER chides his children for being children. God understands that you do not—sometimes cannot—understand what is going on or accept the timing.

Many individuals will try to take away your anger. Don't let them. Some will want you to die "nice." "Now, if you're going to act like this, I'm not going to come around anymore."

You have a right to be angry about leaving the party early, especially if you believe you have things to do. Especially if you have postponed living while "making a living" or becoming a success in your profession. Especially if you have never "been there" for the people who have loved you. No one ever mumbles on a deathbed, "If I could just get in a couple more hours at the office I would feel so much better about dying." Some die angry because they bought into the American canon of success. Dying they recognize how shallow that was. They die angry about the hours away from a family, ball games missed, piano recitals skipped, because of career building. Many will never enjoy that pension, the days in the Florida condo, or strolling along a Maui beach. These fantasies have collapsed. In the words of the Appalachian ballad, "I sold my soul to the company store."

Some are angry at physicians; some are angry at health organizations. Some are angry at insurance companies. Some are angry at the bureaucrats and paper-pushers who complicate dying. Unfortunately, some unleash their anger on the wrong targets, on the closest targets.

Remember the words of Jesus, "My God, my God, why have you forsaken me?" Remember that he summoned all the energy he could to hurl those words at the heavens to provoke a response.

A thought for reflection

If we are attempting to hear God's word, we must listen to anger as carefully as we listen to joy, peace, fear, and fatigue.
—Kathleen Fischer[51]

An audit

I am angry at _____

because _____

_____

I am angry at _____

because _____

_____

I am angry at _____

because _____

_____

I am angry at _____

because _____

_____

I am angry at _____

because _____

_____

A prayer

Hold your anger objects in your mind for a few moments. Then ask God to help you let go of the anger toward that individual.

God, I am owning my anger toward [Name].

I think I have a right to feel angry because [Name] did/said . . . .

What do you think?

What would you have me do with this anger toward [Name]?

Take a moment and think about how [Name] might defend him-self/herself.

Ask God to help you "hear" their defense. When you are ready to let go of this anger, pray:

God, I am ready to let go of this anger toward [Name].

Help me let go of this anger toward [Name].

Breath meditation

Breathe in: The Lord is gracious and compassionate,

Breathe out: slow to anger and rich in love. (Ps 145:8)

Forgiving

Jesus did not pretend that the past had never happened, but He seemed to find ways of not letting it be the end.
—Celtic Daily Prayer[52]

November 1993 was a nightmare for Cardinal Joseph Bernardin. A media fury erupted when Steven Cook, a former seminarian, accused the Cardinal of sexually abusing him. Within hours the accusation and lawsuit were known around the world and a dark cloud billowed over the Cardinal.

Although Cook eventually recanted, Bernardin termed the experience "a profound education of the soul," act one in his spiritual pilgrimage (inoperable cancer being act two). Still Bernardin felt that the incident could not be concluded "until I followed my shepherd's call" to seek out the accuser for reconciliation.

Bernardin met with Cook and his companion and received an apology. Using a century-old chalice, given to him specifically for the occasion, Bernardin celebrated mass and anointed Steven with the sacrament of the sick. Bernardin later wrote about the inadequacy of words to "describe the power of God's grace at work that afternoon. It was a manifestation of God's love, forgiveness, and healing that I will never forget."[53]

Months later when the Cardinal was diagnosed with pancreatic cancer, one of the first letters he received was from Steven Cook. Because of Bernardin's forgiveness, Cook died fully reconciled with the church.

Is it possible that you and the one who has offended, harmed, or wounded you, or someone you have offended, harmed, or wounded, could experience something of that manifestation of God's love, forgiveness, and healing? Yes.

Your act of initiating forgiveness could spur others into acts of forgiving.

The Presidential campaign in 1968 pitting the sitting Vice President, Hubert H. Humphrey, against former Vice President Richard Nixon had been brutal. Humphrey lost by less than one vote per precinct. In the decade that then passed, Nixon had resigned in disgrace and Humphrey was returned to the Senate by voters in Minnesota.

In 1974 Humphrey, dying with cancer, telephoned Nixon in San Clemente, ostensibly to wish him a happy birthday. (Some of Humphrey's aides could not believe his decision: "If it weren't for him and his tactics, you'd be President!") As the two men talked, their animosity wore off. Nixon vowed to an aide, "He's only got a few days, and I don't care what it takes, but I am going to the funeral."[54]

A dying man's gift of grace to a political enemy opened the door for others, over time, to extend an olive branch to Nixon.

Humphrey could have sent "feelers" out to Nixon implying that if his rival wanted to apologize Humphrey would be receptive or even reciprocate. Rather, Humphrey initiated an act of grace so that the latter years of Nixon's life were as a statesman.

It's easy to insist, "I have a right to feel the way I do," and perhaps you do. But when the light of eternity is appearing under the crack of the door, who cares about being right!

Is there someone you need to forgive? Is there someone toward whom you'd like to take the first step?

A thought for reflection

When you forgive, even your worst enemy, you are a sign of the forgiveness of Christ, who never nurtured hatred in his heart.
—John Paul II[55]

An audit

I need to forgive _____ for _____

I need to forgive _____ for _____

I need to forgive _____ for _____

I need to forgive _____ for _____

I need to forgive _____ for _____

A prayer

This will remain a list unless you invite God to help you forgive.
Grace Giver, examine my heart
and help me forgive as generously
as I have been forgiven.
Help me take advantage
of any opportunities for forgiveness
life offers today.

Breath meditation

Breathe in:	And forgive us our trespasses
Breathe out:	as we also forgive those who trespass against us.

Befriending your fears

If God can be found in all things, then there is nothing at all that can happen to us that we need fear.
—*Margaret Hebblethwaite[56]*

Certainly, people have death fears, but more are afraid of *dying* than death itself. Others are afraid of what comes after death. Some have great confidence in Jesus' words, "Do not let your hearts be troubled. . . . I am indeed going to prepare a place for you. And if I go and prepare a place for you, I will come back and take you to be with me that you also may be where I am" (Jn 14:1, 2d, 3). Those words are easy to quote, but some have a difficult time believing that they are included in grace.

We fear eternity is like a "You're a Grand Prize Winner!" notification call. "Congratulations! You've won five glorious days in . . ." only to discover there are lots of strings attached. You've got to sit through a four-hour sales pitch for a condo development.

Some of the most incredible words in scripture are, *"that where I am you also may be."* While scripture says there are no tears in heaven, I suspect there is a lot of bruising from pinching oneself to make sure it's true. Mick Betancourt captures the fear of those who believe in eternal life, but are uncertain they'll get the grand prize:

> I'm afraid that when I die and go to Heaven, I'll
> walk in and the lights will be off. All of a sudden
> the lights come on and all my dead relatives yell,
> "Surprise!!!" As I'm crying with overflowing joy,
> the Devil walks out and says, "That trick never
> gets old. All right you bastards, back to work!"[57]

You wince at the use of the word bastard. But many fear that they are illegitimate children of God, the black sheep he will not acknowledge.

Will Campbell, a colorful and, at times, controversial Southern clergyman who had a way with words, was once challenged, "In ten words or less, what's the Christian message?"

Without blinking an eye Campbell responded, "We're all bastards but God loves us anyway."[58]

Some of us have such vivid hell videos playing on the big screens of our minds. Some have never been able fully to trust God's gracious invitation. We imagine Saint Peter with all the showmanship of a basketball referee growling, "You're out of here!"

My friend Myra, a Jewish rabbi, was asked to come to the hospital to talk to a dying religious who was terrorized by death.

"Shouldn't she talk to a priest?" Myra replied, anxious to avoid any controversy.

"She won't talk to a priest!"

Myra went and after a few minutes asked the dying nun to describe her fears.

"I am afraid God won't accept me into heaven."

"You've been a nun for forty-five years! I'd think you would breeze through central processing."

"But I didn't have pure motives for becoming a nun. And now I am afraid God will turn me away. God knows the truth!" Myra sat with the words, quietly reflecting.

"When I was fourteen my brother raped me. I never told anyone. I entered the convent more as an escape than as a true call to religious life. I have been a hypocrite all these years. Rabbi, you are the first person I've ever told."

Sister feared that the God whom she had so faithfully served would finally settle the score. Myra took the nun's hand.

"I cannot imagine God turning you away. God understands this awful thing that happened to you. God has been with you in this life."

"Yes, but I never forgave my brother. So, I have had sin in my heart all these years."

"Then ask God to help you ask for forgiveness for holding this to your heart."

In a quiet hospital room, a nun found peace. She died several hours later.

Fear can be like an iceberg. There is the portion above the waterline, visible; lurking below the water is the lethal dimension that makes it difficult for some to sense God's outrageously extravagant grace.

I have cherished words sent to me by a therapist friend, Sharon Matthews, "It is good to have available for other things the space that fear takes up in our lives." Think a moment: How much space do your death-related fears take up?

Other fears dismay the dying:

- Fear of the unknown
- Fear of dying in intense pain
- Fear of losing control
- Fear of leaving a family in financial devastation
- Fear of angering God
- Fear of being abandoned by friends who cannot deal with dying
- Fear of nonexistence
- Fear of unfinished business with friends, family members
- Fear of being alone at the hour of death
- Fear of. . . . You fill in the blank.

Stop! Do not read another word. Name your greatest fear to God.

Remember your fears as a child in a dark bedroom. Remember those times you were certain that a monster lurked under your bed? Do you remember your mother showing you that there was no monster under your bed? Let God hear you name the fear. Let God say to you, "Do not be afraid," words God has whispered to all the great personalities of faith throughout history.

The good news is that God wants to come into your fear. God and fear cannot occupy the same space. I like the way one young boy expressed God's care, "I'm not afraid of mice anymore because God gave me a non-afraid feeling." Let God give you a non-afraid feeling.

Remember God's words to Saint Joseph after he discovered his betrothed was pregnant, "Joseph son of David, *do not be afraid* to take Mary home as your wife" (Mt 1:20). Those four words—do not be afraid—occur dozens of times in scripture. Surely that was not the last of Joseph's fears. Think what he must have experienced as he and Mary fled Bethlehem in the night for safety in Egypt.

The same God who spoke those words to Joseph in a dream two millennia ago would speak equally empowering words to you, "Do not be afraid." Part of the joy of eternal life will be the absence of even a molecule of fear.

If you can't evict fear outrightly, be a menacing landlord. Fear will move out on its own.

A thought for reflection

I stand anchored now in God
before whom I stand naked,
this God who tells me,
"You are my son, my beloved one."
—John Eagan[59]

An audit

Think about your fears. Name them.
I fear _____ _____
I fear _____
I fear _____
I fear _____
I fear _____ ____
I fear _____

A prayer

God, my fears are not hidden from you.
Give me sufficient courage to face them
in the light of your love.

Breath meditation

Breathe in: Do not let your hearts be troubled

Breathe out: and do not be afraid. (Jn 14:27)

Deciding how you want to be remembered

We can't accept the fact that our lives will pass and we left no mark on the world.
—Harold Kushner[60]

Many dying persons fear being forgotten more than they fear death. "What ever happened to so-and-so?" is too common a question. Alfred had quite a scare. When his brother Ludwig died, a mistake was made and Alfred's obituary was published. His obituary described him as "the merchant of death" because so many people had died as a result of his invention: dynamite.

The French journalist writing the obituary got the brothers confused and reported Alfred's death. The unfavorable obituary gave the inventor an opportunity to challenge his remembrance by leaving nine million dollars to underwrite the Nobel Peace Prizes.[61]

How do you want to be remembered? Whom do you want to remember you? Even Jesus, facing death, had questions about how he would be remembered. In his last meal Jesus lifted the cup and pleaded, "This cup is the new covenant in my blood; do this, whenever you drink it, *in remembrance of me*" (1 Cor 11:25). Within hours, one disciple had betrayed him, three had fallen asleep while he agonized in Gethsemane, one denied him around a fire, and one fled naked. Not exactly the men you want planning a memorial.

Some people stun friends with a generous gift to an educational or charitable institution. Others provide resources for someone to pursue a dream. For example, my master's degree was paid for by a couple I never met, Ed and Gladys Hurley. Given the number of student loans I had from undergraduate school, graduate work would have been impossible without their generosity.

But there are other more intangible ways to be remembered. There will be friends who will say, "I will always remember the time you. . . . I will not forget how you. . . ."

That's a reason to have a vigil. People come bearing not only condolences but also remembrances and stories they can tell only after your death because you would have dismissed the telling, "Oh, it wasn't anything special. . . ."

That's one reason to have a eulogist "recollect" you—to jump-start memories within those who attend your funeral, memorial service, or wake. Some will remember you from recent days, others will remember you from childhood, or high school, or a special project in your parish or your first job. Your family may never have met these individuals, but their stories will contribute to the memory mix.

An individual is not dead until two things happen: Survivors stop saying their names *and* stop telling stories about them. Give people whose lives you have touched an opportunity to gather to tell and to exchange stories about you.

Chicago sportscaster Harry Caray will long be remembered for his gravely voice, oversized glasses, and that distinctive, "Holy Cow!" uttered during Cubs baseball games. When Caray died in 1998, people wondered, "How do you ritualize someone 'bigger than life'?" At Harry's funeral in Chicago's Holy Name Cathedral, priests cracked jokes and friends roasted the colorful baseball broadcaster not only for his "love and tireless commitment to the fans" but also for his "passion for alcohol and a night at the bars."[62] They remembered the real Harry Caray.

Nobel discovered that he didn't have to die the way he had lived. Dying has a way of making individuals who cooperate more kind, more tenderhearted, more compassionate, more caring. Dying can give you time to sand down some rough edges, to smooth out some wrinkles.

A thought for reflection

People don't leave until you stop thinking about them.
—Larry McMurtry[63]

An audit

Take some time to reflect on how you want to be remembered.

I want to be remembered for _____

I want to be remembered for _____

I want to be remembered for _____

I want to be remembered for _____

I especially want to be remembered by _____

Breath meditation

Breathe in: Jesus, remember me

Breath out: when you come into your kingdom.
                   (Lk 23:42)

Reviewing your life

When it's over, I don't want to wonder if I have made of my life something particular, and real. I don't want to find myself sighing and frightened, or full of argument. I don't want to end up simply having visited this world.
—Mary Oliver[64]

You've probably used, or heard, the expression, "I saw my life pass before my eyes." Dying offers some a chance to watch old videos the way a coach studies videos from previous games. Those videos have lessons to teach us—if we are willing to look closely for the clues.

For many people the amount of financial assets left is the criteria for evaluating a life: "He left them very well off!" Words attributed to Ralph Waldo Emerson offer an alternative.

To laugh often and much;

To win the respect of intelligent people and the
affection of children;

To earn the appreciation of honest critics and
endure the betrayal of false friends;

To appreciate beauty, to find the best in others;

To leave the world a little better, whether by a
healthy child, a garden patch or a redeemed
social condition;

To know even one life has breathed easier because
you have lived;

This is to have succeeded.[65]

Hang out with these words. Underline the phrase in this quote that grabs your attention. Have you lived in such a way that your eulogist(s) will be frustrated because there is not enough time to cover all the good about you?

Admittedly, there are shadows and dark spots you want to exclude. However, those places and spaces are part of your story; in fact, you have only become you by surviving them.

Time to make amends. One of the important elements of the Twelve Steps is Step Four: "make a thorough and fearless inventory of our life." "AA-ers" know the power of confession: it liberates the soul from maintaining false self-images. It works like a giant plunger on the backwash of the soul.

Now might be a time to let go of some of the claim tickets to justice you have been holding on to, some worn and frayed. You may want to make some phone calls or write some letters. You may want to see certain people, or invite them to come to you.

The church has long offered the Sacrament of Reconciliation. You can extend the grace received from the sacrament to others. Saint Francis captured the reality, "for it is in giving, that we receive; it is in pardoning, that we are pardoned." Even if you believe you have a right to feel the way you do, do you want to die clutching that right?

Ten words could impact your death and the grief of those who survive you.

I am sorry.

I was wrong.

Will you forgive me?

Admittedly, the first six words are easier to verbalize; in fact, we can mumble them in an off-hand way that infers, "But you were *more* wrong."

Life reviews have pluses *and* minuses. In Judaism, *hesped* is a balanced eulogy. The bottom line before death may not make the scales balance. Sometimes, it takes stories at a vigil to tip the audit to the positive column.

I read obituaries with great interest. I would like to have known Florence McNaul Mueller because of her obituary:

> Although she and her husband worked full time in the family business, she always had time for her children and their friends. Although she was a den mother and home room mother, Florence was the one teachers looked to if kids needed to be transported . . . if food needed to be prepared . . . if an event needed to be hosted.
>
> She opened her home to her children's friends and hosted innumerable sleepovers for 20, 30, and

40 kids at a time. . . . She made certain that her house was the place everyone wanted to be . . . known by all for her sense of humor and her spirit for living. . . . Florence Mueller, in her last words to the family, gave a great life review, "We sure had fun, didn't we?"[66]

A thought for reflection

Today may be a good time to "get around to" what you've been meaning to get around to.

An audit

Too many obituaries are little more than the equivalent of "name, rank, and serial number." If you write your obituary—or an early draft—you are giving your family a gift. In a hundred words or less, "obituary" your life.

_____

_____

_____

_____

_____

_____

A prayer

Jesus, friend of sinners,
    listen to my prayer, forgive all my sins,
    renew your love in my heart,
    and bring me peace.

Help me to live all the days remaining in my life
    in harmony with my fellow Christians—
    family—friends—neighbors—medical personnel
    that I may live out your saving and sustaining power
    to all the world. Amen.[67]

Breath meditation

Breathe in: May the Lord bless me

Breathe out: all the days of my life. (Ps 128:5)

Making room in your dying for some living

There is no box made by God nor us but that the sides can be flattened out and the top blown off to make a dance floor on which to celebrate life.
—Keith Caraway[68]

My father amazed me in the months before he died. Whenever I asked, "Daddy, how are you?" he answered, "Still a-kickin'!"

The real danger is dying before you die. The question is not "Is there life after death?" but rather, "Is there life *during* life?" There are individuals who died twenty years ago who are just now getting around to being ritualized and buried.

You probably know someone who has heard the diagnosis and died within a few days or weeks. I heard Dr. Bernie Siegel, then an oncologist at Yale Medical School, tell an intriguing story at

Temple B'nai Jehudah about a patient who said surgery was inconvenient. Siegel tried to scare him, "I am offering you a chance to live. This is your *only* chance to live."

"Doc, this is not a good time. I have things to do."

"You do not have any choice! If you don't let me operate, you'll be dead in three months!"

The man did not have the surgery. Years passed. One day, Siegel noticed the name on a chart and thought it coincidental that two persons had the same name. He was stunned to find the same patient sitting in an exam room.

"You're alive!" Siegel exclaimed, glancing at the date he had last seen the man.

"Yeah, I had some questions and I thought I ought to come in to see you."

"Well, what do you want to ask?"

"What do you think a man in my condition should be eating?"

"'In your condition?' If you have lived this long, you can eat *anything* you want!"

The man grinned. "You know, Dr. Siegel, I felt bad telling you that I couldn't have surgery. But you see, I am a gardener, and if you recall, that was spring, and I needed to plant flowers and my garden. Then I had to look after my garden . . . and time just got away from me."[69]

Obviously, this man made room in his dying for grand living. Lots of living.

Any time line offered by a physician is a "guesstimate." In the Old Testament, King Hezekiah, when told he had a fatal disease, turned to the wall and prayed, "Remember, O Lord, how I have walked before you faithfully and with wholehearted devotion and have done what is good in your eyes." Then he "wept bitterly" (2 Kings 20:3).

The Lord heard his prayer and granted Hezekiah fifteen more years of life. In your anguished moments when you turn your face to the wall, remember God will hear your prayers and see your tears. You may not get fifteen years like Hezekiah, but you will get life until you die.

I served as an admissions officer at a university with a visionary president. Shelburne Brown had orchestrated a move from a land-locked campus in Pasadena to a spectacular coastal campus along the Pacific in San Diego. Just as the wisdom of his leadership was becoming evident, he was diagnosed with an inoperable brain tumor. Weeks later during Christmas vacation a student was killed in an avalanche while mountain climbing. The memorial chapel service was hushed as Dr. Brown spoke.

"Obviously, I'm *still* here. You've been praying for me to live because I have a terminal diagnosis. But none of you have been praying for Tami, because, as students, you think you're invincible. Your lives are ahead of you. This is the irony of life: I am here, Tami is gone. My advice is to live today." Shelburne Brown took his own advice.

Months before he died, a friend and I took Dr. Brown, now blind, to a San Diego Padres baseball game. I was concerned about navigating a zillion steps guiding him, but it turned out to be a glorious night in the ballpark. Driving back to his condo, I spotted a Baskin-Robbins.

"Dr. Brown, how about an ice cream cone? I'll buy!"

On a hot July night we sat in the parking lot enjoying ice cream and talking about how good life was. I will never forget his appreciation for an ice cream cone, "Man, this is good ice cream!" Back at his condo, he paused before getting out of the car.

"I had a great time. Thank you for asking me to go with you." Dr. Brown had to give up his passions for piloting and for golfing, but he made room for other joys in his dying season.

Although death is every human's eventual reality, wise teachers from across the religious spectrum counsel to live in the present moment. *Carpe diem*. Don't squander *this* day. Live!

If you decide to live outrageously, today could be a day to create a memory that will be treasured for eternity.

A thought for reflection

Do not stop thinking of life as an adventure.

You have no security unless you can live bravely, excitingly, imaginatively!

—Eleanor Roosevelt[70]

An audit

In this day the Lord has given me
   I can live bravely by _____
   I can live bravely by _____

In this day the Lord has given me
   I can live excitingly by _____
   I can live excitingly by _____

In this day the Lord has given me
   I can live imaginatively by _____
   I can live imaginatively by _____

Breath meditation:

Breathe in: This is the day the Lord has made;

Breathe out: I will rejoice and be glad in it! (Ps 118:24)

Making doxologies

For what has been—thanks! For what shall be—yes!
—Dag Hammarskjold[71]

Simple things make a difference. Simple acts of kindness may come from unexpected sources.

The ability to say "thank you" to life, to God, to family members, to nurses, doctors, orderlies, to recognize acts of kindness, is to make room for doxologizing. A thank-you becomes a word of praise for God. A key result of a good life review is identifying gifts for which to express gratitude. Saint Paul, who faced death on several occasions, urged, "let the peace of Christ rule in your hearts" and "Be thankful." Gratitude is a key element in navigating last days.

Gratitude starts with small things. Gratitude starts with a decision on your part to voice thankfulness. Say "thank you" often—even if you have to rehearse it. One dying man said, "It is about being thankful that I can still do x, y, z—even though I could once do a-z."

William G. Bartholome, a pediatrician at Kansas University Medical School, was featured in Bill Moyers' PBS special on death and dying. His essay, "A Prayer," something of a Christmas letter reviewing his four-year "battle" or learning experience with cancer, was punctuated with seven "thank-yous."

> Thank you, God, for my partner, my wife.
> Thank you, God, for my parents, my siblings, my
> children, my web of being.
> Thank you, God, for this opportunity to be truly
> alive.
> Thank you, God, for this opportunity to guide.
> Thank you, God, for giving us this gift of
> life/death.
> Thank you, God, for bringing me back into your
> presence.
> Thank you, God, for this great gift.

I find the last paragraph of his Christmas letter amazing: "I have been so blessed. You cannot possibly know the depth of my gratitude at having had these precious years to share with you."[72]

You may protest, "Wait a minute. This guy is dying!" It is not unlike the milk glass: is it half full or half empty? It is a matter of perspective. Bartholome chose to see the glass as half full.

Gratitude is the most effective antidote for self-pity.

A thought for reflection

When we are struck by personal tragedy, often the only way to get a perspective is by focusing on that for which we all have to be grateful.

—Mark Schel[73]

An audit

Using Bill Bartholome's pattern, create your personal doxology, praising God through offering thanks.

Thank you, God, for _____.

Thank you, God, for _____.

Thank you, God, for _____.

Thank you, God, for this opportunity to _____.

Thank you, God, for giving me this gift of _____.

Thank you, God, for bringing me _____.

Thank you, God, for _____.

A prayer

God, forgive me for all the times
I have offered pathetic, anemic "thank-yous."
Forgive me for all the times
I have not appreciated your good gifts.
Give me a grateful heart.

Breath meditation

Breathe in: I will bless the Lord

Breathe out: at all times! (Ps 34:1)

Making life easier for your survivors

All too often the process of staying alive destroys the process of being alive.
—Ted Menton[74]

By dealing forthrightly with death, you make life easier for those who will have to learn to live without you. It is your choice. One piece of wisdom I have long appreciated is: "It is not so much what happens to you, as it is a question of how you choose to respond." That's why denial is not an option.

Pam Bartholome said it well, "His suffering is not just his suffering— it is *our* suffering. The person who is dying cannot die alone. The caregiver cannot do this alone. There must be support somewhere."[75] One way we make life easier for those who will have to learn to live without us is to include them in the dying. If our support team is limited to a spouse or a child, their ability to meet all the needs is going to be impaired.

Some get "dress rehearsals" for death; others get only the final performance. Bartholome asked, "Help me have the best experience of my death that I can." The goal is to improve the quality of one's living until dying.

A thought for reflection

I do not choose to be a common man,
it is my God-given right to be uncommon.
—Inscription on grave marker of Lee Atwater

An audit

Today, I can make my dying easier on _____
by _____
Today, I can make my dying easier on _____
by _____
Today, I can make my dying easier on _____
by _____
Today, I can make my dying easier on _____
by _____

A prayer

God, you have given me such a supportive family.
You have given me so many amazing friends.
You have given me so many people to love.
You have given me love through so many individuals.
Would you prepare their hearts
to receive your consolation and peace
when I can no longer say to them, "I love you."

Breath meditation

Breathe in: God will wipe away

Breathe out: every tear from their eyes. (Rv 7:17)

Making a valid will

If you neglect to create a will, the state has one waiting for you.
—Andy Morrison[76]

You do not know what kind of family you are in until you settle an estate. An estimated three-fourths of Americans die without a will, a valid will, or without an updated will; many die without a will that adequately reflects their last "last wishes."

I have never been able to forget the headline in *The Kansas City Star*, "Burger Left 'Inadequate' Will, and It Could Cost Heirs a Lot." Although Warren Burger was Chief Justice of the U.S. Supreme Court, 1969-1986, he wrote a "woefully inadequate" will after the death of his wife that resulted in major complications for his heirs. Apparently, the Chief Justice wrote the will hastily, did not check spelling, and did not grant his executors power to sell his real estate. So, the heirs had to go to court to obtain that permission.[77]

When have you last reviewed your will? When you reviewed your will, did you sign and date it? Does it accommodate your current relationships? Does it best distribute your assets? Does it take advantage of current tax options? In the words of the head-line, will your will cost your heirs a lot of time and money?

Many people describe themselves as pro-family. The best lit-mus test is an up-to-date will. If you die intestate, there could be a financial nightmare for those you love. If you don't like paying taxes, think how you'll rest in eternity knowing the state "took" a significant portion of your estate to pave a stretch of highway or buy toilet tissue.

And guess what? Your family won't like it!

Not having a will sabotages and complicates your loved one's grief. They will, of necessity, spend time and money in an attorney's office as they survive the legal and financial maze. They will expend incredible emotional, and perhaps financial, capital trying to settle your estate.

Secrets, surprises, and sabotages! Some families have open conversations and relationships; others rely on assumptions and falsehoods. In one sense, it's only money, but money has a way of undermining relationships—not just in this generation but in future generations, too.

Admittedly, some draw up wills while angry at a particular individual. Nevertheless that is your last will. You have a right to divide your possessions as you wish. But, if you wish to be gener-ous to one child, how will that generosity be understood by oth-ers in the family (including in-laws) and by future generations?

One gift you may want to consider giving is a Committee of the Family. Call your family together and disclose the contents of your will. That way there will be no surprises, although there may be disagreement on provisions.

Possessions can be enriched or de-riched by individuals; other issues get reactivated in the dividing up process. "He always liked you more than he liked me. . . ."

The longer you delay, the potentially more complicated the settling estate can be. The more unsettling the estate, the more unsettling is your family's future relationships.

Remember, it may not be things like boats, stocks, houses, or art that launch a battle. It could be a pickle dish, a punch bowl. All it will take is a "...but I just know that he wanted me to have it!" to undermine the good will of a family. None of your heirs may snarl, "Over my dead body . . . " but you can limit the potential skirmishes by making wishes known clearly. Small emotionally laden possessions can lead to large legal, emotional, and sometimes physical slug-fests.

Recheck beneficiaries. Have you overlooked any insurance policies? If you divorced and remarried, did you change your beneficiary on all life insurance policies including those an employer or fraternal organization carries? By naming a beneficiary, that asset is removed from the estate.

Executor(s). Is your executor(s) still willing to serve? Is your named executor still alive? Locate-able? Competent? Is there any degree of hesitancy on her or his part? Has anything changed in the mental or financial ability of the executor? Given the mobility in this country, in some states an executor is required to reside in the state. This individual will be charged with making sense of your wishes without your being around to supervise. Do you trust your executor implicitly?

Tell your loved ones where your will can be found.

A thought for reflection

Only with a will can you control exactly who will get what, when, and how.

—Andy Morrison[78]

An audit

One important function of an executor is to inventory the estate. One act before "passing on" a treasure is to take a moment and express gratitude to God for these possessions.

Physically—or if you are unable to do so physically, mentally—wander around your residence and notice what you would consider "treasures." With a particular item, take a moment and recount how that came into your possession.

Are there items that need to be returned to a "rightful" owner?

Spend some time giving thanks for the treasures.

Spend some time imagining it with a new owner.

A prayer

God, would you guide me
in passing on to friends, family,
especially the next generation,
these items that have been important to me,
that have been so much a part of my life.
Help me give these gifts in such a way
that they will become a blessing to the recipients.

Breath meditation

Breathe in: Remember the Lord your God,

Breathe out: he has given you the ability to produce
                     wealth. (Dt 8:18)

Giving it to them now!

Yesterday is history. Tomorrow is mystery. Today is a gift!
—Eleanor Roosevelt[79]

Billy knew that his diagnosis would lead to an early death. Once when I was visiting, he held up a beautiful piece of glass and promised, "This will be yours after I die." I must have looked surprised because he added, "I'd give it to you now, but . . . I'm not through dusting it yet." Then he laughed.

Weeks after he died, the object arrived in the mail and now sits on my dining room buffet. While he did not turn over actual custody of the items, he did, in a moment, give them to me.

By giving assets now you gain three benefits:

You get to experience the exchange. The look on the recipient's face, their words will warm you.

You know the items went to the person you wanted to have them. Yes, they probably will get to the desired owner after your death, but snafus happen. In some families, certain things "disappear."

You can link the item to a story. Do you have a story to tell about the item that will be treasured and passed on? Some items become a major part of the family lore. Stories get jump-started with "Where did you get that?" Many individuals have "stuff" but also have questions about where it came from or how it came into the loved one's possession. Unfortunately, the only person who knew the story, or more than a hazy inkling of details, is unable to supply them. A lot of the history of treasured objects gets lost over time.

Beatrice Ash suggests that we visualize loved ones owning and using favorite possessions. Thus, we see the transfer in our mind's eye. When Dorothy, an older woman dying of cancer, said to Beatrice, "I hope I've made my wishes clear to my lawyer," Ash recognized the hesitancy. So, she suggested giving away items while she was still living. "Oh, it would make people uncomfortable."

Dorothy agreed to try. When a friend dropped by, Dorothy seized the opportunity. Soon, she began inviting friends for tea "and made a private, meaningful ceremony of giving the gifts she had planned to have her attorney distribute. In so doing, she gave a part of herself in the form of special memories to her friends."[80] Moreover, she reduced her attorney's billable hours against the estate.

Practice this statement, "I want you to have this. *Now.*" Then add, "Because. . . ." If you give it to them now, they have to dust it and take care of it (and, in some cases, insure it), but it reduces one item for your executor to have to deal with. My friend Billy, in addition to his will, left six legal page notes of disbursement: "This goes to. . . ." His mother has spent a lot of time wrapping, packing, and shipping.

A thought for reflection

Whatever you do to physically provide for your loved ones will have everything to do with how they cope emotionally after you're gone.

—Beatrice Ash[81]

An audit

Today I will do something to make my executor's job easier.
I can _____

Today I will do something to make my executor's job easier.
I can _____

Today I will do something to make my executor's job easier.
I can _____

A prayer

God, if I have to die now,
help me make the best of this passage
into your everlasting kingdom.

Breath meditation

Breathe in: Because of the Lord's compassion

Breathe out: I am not consumed. (Lam 3:22)

Guarding the gate

One duty of a door-keeper is to stand guard against all that is
harmful; another is to welcome whoever may come as a guest.
—The Celtic Daily Prayer[82]

Many dying persons have a "gatekeeper" who decides who gets access and who does not. Have you appointed a gatekeeper? Has someone volunteered to take on the responsibility? Some gatekeepers go overboard. The family of Eleanor Roosevelt rigidly enforced the "no visitors" code as the former First Lady lay dying in a New York City hospital.

Even Adlai Stevenson, a devoted friend, was denied access. "But I am her friend," protested the man whose campaigns for president in 1952 and 1956 had been orchestrated behind the scenes by Mrs. Roosevelt. Stevenson and others were pointedly informed that the former First Lady did not want to be seen "in her invalid condition."

Ambassador Stevenson, a skilled negotiator, pleaded with the family for "just a few moments" with his friend. Finally, daughter Anna gave in. "Come, if you would like, but I don't think she will recognize you." Stevenson had to settle for waving from the doorway.[83]

If you relinquish control on this point, someone will make decisions which may deny access to you.

Carly Simon recounts the call that she had been dreading from Marta Sgubin, Jackie Kennedy Onassis's housekeeper, "Caroline says you should come over now." Simon found lots of friends and family present in Mrs. Onassis's apartment, but discovered that Jackie's last wishes had been that only "a few women friends outside the family" see her as she died. Carly felt privileged that Caroline and John recognized the strength of her friendship with their mother. In a low, comforting voice, Carly spoke to Jackie telling her how much she loved her. "During that time I was sitting with Jackie and holding her hand, I felt as though I had direct communication with her—an experience that was deep, personal, and untainted by self-consciousness."[84]

This was Jackie Onassis's gift to Carly Simon. You can offer this gift of final presence to your friends.

Because she was given access to her friend, Carly Simon's grief was not hamstrung as was Stevenson's. Give your friends an opportunity to say goodbye. You are not helping them by keeping them at arm's length. They need to see, sense, and smell death close up.

I find a link to the Holy Family. The visitors to the stable in Bethlehem came bearing gifts—resources that would be needed for the family's journey with this special child of God.

Visitors come bearing "gifts" for your journey, too. They may bring reminders of experiences that you have forgotten. They may bring ingredients for your life review. They may bring words of affirmation that only they can give.

A thought for reflection

Be careful in selecting a gatekeeper. Power in the wrong hands, even in well-meaning hands, can make for a lonely dying for you.

An audit

Ask yourself: Who do I want to see? Who do I *not* want to see?

I want to see _____

I want to see _____

I want to see _____

I do not want to see _____

I do not want to see _____

I do not want to see _____

A prayer

God, how many times have you welcomed me into your presence? Give me strength to be a host to those you wish to bring to me.

Breath meditation

Breathe in: The Lord is good to all;

Breathe out: he has compassion on all he has made.
(Ps 145:9)

Offering hospitality

Hospitality is about a relationship—one cannot be hospitable
without guests.
—Matthew Fox[85]

Queen Elizabeth II has a practice of sending invitations to tradesmen asking them to come talk with her. It's called an audience. Imagine the world's richest woman sitting comfortably chatting with plumbers, electricians, and construction workers, but this offers the queen a way to keep up with what is going on in the kingdom. So, who would you summon for an audience?

Admittedly, some people get stimulus-overload in visiting a sick room or hospital. A scent or smell in your room can trigger a strong memory from another's sick room—a memory they have suppressed.

In candle shops, I have found all kinds of scents but never "hospital." Hospitals have their own distinct smells. Individuals, because of their illnesses and the chemicals they are being treated with (and their bodies' reaction to the chemicals), produce more odors.

Sometimes, you may want to see this reality as an opportunity. Candles with the aroma of pumpkin pie, fresh cookies, and fresh cut grass not only hide smells but also stimulate memories and stories. You may prefer incense. Or the little aroma rims that sit on light bulbs. Explore aromatherapy, particularly scents such as chamomile, lavender, rose, and geranium. Try aerosol sprays (always in moderation).

Particular scents may be positive triggers. One dying teenager found the smell of baby powder comforting—a scent from childhood memories. One family brought evergreens into the home to evoke memories of previous Christmases. Fresh cookies may not only be eaten but the aroma can comfort. Identify your comfort scents and use them as provisions for the journey.

Hold court. By the time John was through redecorating, it didn't look like a hospital room. It was his space. Although hospitals create homey birthing suites, patients die in some of the most cramped, cluttered spaces. Who designs these rooms? Certainly not dying people or their loved ones. Why not dying suites?

Make the best of it. It may be easier to die in a manor house with maids to bring refreshments to guests. Sometimes, a cup of coffee has power to break the ice—to make someone comfortable. Is there something you can offer?

You could hardly get in the door of my mother's home before she asked, "Are you hungry? Do you want something to eat? I just made. . . ." My mother was always "tickled" when people came to visit. Eventually, as Alzheimer's governed her life, people still came although she didn't know them or remember the visit.

One of my best "toward-the-end" memories is the two of us devouring a box of Russell Stover candy one afternoon. Mother did not know who I was, but she did know Russell Stover. "That is the best candy," she said. "I think I will have another piece." She offered the only hospitality she could: Russell Stover candy.

Show hospitality by offering what you have: you.

A thought for reflection

We must be ready to allow ourselves to be interrupted by God. God will constantly be crossing our paths and canceling our plans by sending us people with claims and petitions.

—Dietrich Bonhoeffer[86]

A prayer

Jesus, you promised that where two or three are gathered
   you, too, would be present.
Give grace to those who are hesitant, afraid, fearful of saying
   the wrong thing to me.
Give me grace to offer hospitality to all who come to me.

Breath meditation

Breathe in: You prepare a table before me

Breathe out: in the presence of my enemies. (Ps 23:5)

Making visitors comfortable

The living and the dying are in the same resort. The dying may be checking out sooner than the healthy. But make no mistake, everyone will check out.

Sometimes conversation between the dying and the not-dying-at-the-moment resembles the awkwardness of junior high students learning to dance. Fortunately, they do not give up; they keep dancing. So we should keep talking.

If you are uncomfortable with dying, your visitors are going to be uncomfortable. However, if you can see a visit as a "teachable" moment, who knows what might come out of a visit?

Some visitors will try to skirt the big issues. Visitors will not only want to deny death, but to deny your death. If it can happen to you, it can happen to them.

Some will bob and prance like boxers trying to avoid the punch. They keep the conversation "light." You want to say, "Excuse me, but I am dying!" With some you will have a feeling they are talking at you rather than with you. With others long awkward silences prevail. You may need sentences like the following to get a conversation "rolling."

"I am getting good care."

"I am learning that the best medicine is people letting me know that I am still valued."

"I am glad that I do not have to go through this alone."

A thought for reflection

Your need to feel connected to other people is as vital to human survival as food, water, and shelter.

—Morrie Schwartz[87]

An audit

If you could choose any five people in the world to visit you now, who would you choose? Why

I would choose _____ because _____

_____

I would choose _____ because _____

_____

I would choose _____ because _____

_____

I would choose _____ because _____

_____

I would choose _____ because _____

_____

A prayer

God, how do I make visitors comfortable?
What do I have to offer them?
Help me to recognize and appreciate
    the gifts they bring.
Make this space a safe place to say "goodbye."

Breath meditation

Breathe in: O Lord, I call to you;

Breathe out: come quickly to me. (Ps 141:1)

Ignoring the well-intentioned

Had it not been for Nightline, Morrie might have died without ever seeing me again. I had no good excuse for this, except the one that everyone these days seems to have. I had become too wrapped up in the siren song of my own life. I was busy.
—Mitch Albom[88]

Art Linkletter made a name for himself with the television show and book *Kids Say the Darndest Things!* Well, it's not only kids! People who visit the dying can make children seem amateurish. Because people do not know what to say, or think they have to say something, they say the most outrageous things!

"You're looking better." (Better get your eyes checked.)

"You seem better today." (Better check at the nurses' station.)

In scripture, as Job suffered, friends came to offer "comfort." For seven days and seven nights they sat with him in silence. Then they opened their mouths and blew the opportunity to be remembered as brilliant, sensitive role models.

There will be people you wish will leave and stay away.

There will be some you wish wouldn't stay so long.

There will be some you wish would get real.

So, what can you do to keep from feeling resentful?

Pray for them. Job had to endure his "comforters." Yet a remarkable observation can be found in the last chapter of Job's epic, "After Job had prayed for his friends, the Lord made him prosperous again" (Job 42:10). Use Jesus' guidance, "Forgive them, for they do not know what they are doing" (Lk 23:34) or saying.

Bless them. You can make an opportunity to "bless" your friends. Your dying may leave them so vulnerable, so afraid that their compassion index will be low. Your last moments with them can be an unforgettable experience.

The last time I saw Twila Arbuckle I prayed with her just as I had prayed for her, her husband, and two sons. Sensing it might be our last conversation, I asked Twila to pray *for* me. I will never forget her "blessing" me.

You can start with the words Jacob used, dying, to bless his two Egyptian grandsons.

> May the God before whom my fathers
> > Abraham and Isaac walked,
> the God who has been my shepherd
> > all my life to this day,
> the Angel who has delivered me from all harm
> > —may he bless these boys.
> > > —Genesis 48:15-16

Give them some ideas of what you would like to hear. Make the visit a tutorial like Professor Morrie did. Morrie taught Mitch Albom to be more at ease with dying. Through his best-seller, *Tuesdays with Morrie*, Albom has taught millions of readers to be more caring. You can make a difference in lives long after your death. It would be helpful if a website offered ten "helpful" things to say while visiting a dying person. In the meantime, seize the opportunity and train visitors. Write on a sheet of paper, "Here are some things I am willing to talk about and some things I am anxious to talk about."

Be willing to confront. If a comment or observation annoys you, say so. Challenge the visitor: "[Name] do you have any idea how that sounds to me?" (So what if he gets angry! What will the visitor do— boycott your wake? Go fishing or shopping during your funeral?) This could turn into a life lesson.

Sometimes people keep on saying stupid things because no one ever challenges them, "You know, on the stupid scale, that remark is a 10!"

Catherine was dying. This innovative college dean requested that a priest visit. At some point in their conversation, the young priest confidently said, "I know what you are going through." Her eyes flashed.

"Father, you have no idea what I am going through!" Catherine snapped.

Stunned, Father thought a moment and replied, "You are right. I have no idea." That day he learned a life lesson from a dying woman and eliminated the cliché from his compassion vocabulary.

Amy Porter had a beau, a wedding dress, and a date for a wedding—but she also had cancer. Although buoyed by many people who came to see her, one annoyed her. Finally, she suggested that her father not invite this individual to visit again—a request that puzzled her father until Amy explained, "Well, instead of pleading for my healing, he just kept asking God to please do His will." Amy preferred visitors who prayed more aggressively.

Amy also asked her father to invite a particular friend who seemed to "arm-wrestle with God" in his prayers for Amy. He pleaded like the persistent widow before the unjust judge in Luke's gospel (18:1-5).

Amy died without that storybook ending, "And they lived happily ever after. . . ." But Amy danced with hope until the last breath and her peers never forgot moments spent with her.[89]

A thought for reflection

There is so much more to life than fear of death. Each day is like a gift to enjoy and savor. Oddly enough, in spite of earlier morbid moods, I wouldn't change places with any man.

—Cornelius Ryan[90]

A prayer

I am troubled, O Lord; come to my aid.

—The prayer of King Hezekiah, Isaiah 38:14

Breath meditation

Breathe in: I am troubled, O Lord;

Breathe out: come to my aid. (Is 38:14)

Dealing with the strugglers

I chuckled while reading a story about the humor of Peter Chirchirillo, who died in the World Trade Center bombing. At weekend parties for family and friends, he would teasingly set five alarm clocks to go off at 7:00 p.m. Then, Peter loved to yell, "It's time to go home, everybody. Get out." He turned leaving a party into a great game friends loved.[91]

You will have "struggling" visitors who struggle seeing you this way. I remember massaging Martin just before he died. I was speechless as he pulled off his sweatshirt and T-shirt. The bones protruded through his skin.

"Martin," I swallowed hard, "I am afraid I will hurt you. . . ." He did not let me finish.

"Just touch me. I will tell you if you are hurting me." I prayed that I would remember the lessons I had learned studying with Louise Smith, a recognized innovator of massage for the dying. That afternoon I was a struggler. Martin helped me find a rhythm for my touch and he helped me find my voice. That last conversation was the most open in our friendship. The barriers were down. We both acknowledged that he was dying.

Talk about the "patience of Job." It wasn't only patience with his physical pain but also patience with the barrage of words his visitors unleashed on him.

Friends struggle because you are a mirror; the uglier your dying, the more menacing the reflection, the more fear triggered within them. "This could happen to me!" some think. The first time your friend finds you in diapers can challenge verbal skills.

You will have a high discomfort sensor. You may find yourself angry after someone abruptly leaves. It will be easy to take out that anger on a nurse, a housekeeper, a family member, or the next visitor.

Sometimes you should ask the struggler, "What is it about my dying that makes you uncomfortable?" Hold his feet to the fire if he tries to dance his way out of the conversation. This could be a life-changing moment for the struggler as well as for you.

A thought for reflection

We isolate the dying by no longer talking about what's going on. The widely held notion that the dying do not want to talk about death is a myth. They do want to talk about what is happening to them.

—David Kessler[92]

An audit

If someone would listen without interrupting to the ends of my sentences:

I would like to talk to _____
about _____
I would like to talk to _____
about _____
I would like to talk to _____
about _____

A prayer

God, loosen my tongue and
loosen [Name]'s ears
that they can hear me
as well as you hear me.

Breath meditation

Breathe in: Out of the depths I cry to you,

Breathe out: O Lord, hear my voice. (Ps 130:1-2)

Leaving an ethical will

*I don't think most people realize how powerful their last will and
testament can be—for good or ill.*
—Patricia Weenolsen[93]

Dorothy Culver, at ninety-three, told me that her one regret
was that she would not live to see what Anna, her six-year-old
granddaughter, would grow up to be. "But," Dot reminded me,
"she will be something!" Dot left an incredible gift to Anna, who
more than once "took in" her grandmother's observation. She
knows that her grandmother believed she was going to "make
something" of herself. Anna will.

For centuries fathers and mothers have left not only wills to
divide possessions, but also ethical wills. In the ethical will, long-
ings, hopes, aspirations, affirmations are passed on to the next or
future generations. These wills, according to Rabbis Kerry Olitzky
and Ronald Isaacs,

provide those who come after you with sound advice based on what you have learned from life. It may be possible to have your loved ones learn what you have learned without having to experience some of the challenges you have faced.[94]

Think of it as passing on a legacy. Maybe you are passing on a family business. That is accomplished through the will; the ethical will identifies the values that built the business in the hope others will honor those values.

You could express wishes that your heirs continue a tradition or emulate some of your principles. It is not an attempt to control but rather an effort to pass on core values to which you are committed. Or it can be a look to the future, "John, I hope that you will always continue to be strong and kind, that you remain committed to the needs of the underdog. Meredith, it is my hope that you will devote more time to pursuing your artistic talents."

This gift of blessing through an ethical will traces back to words that the dying patriarch Jacob used to "bless" his sons. On his death bed, Jacob gave each son "the blessing appropriate to him" (Gn 49:28).

You may decide to read and discuss the provisions of the ethical will before death. You may tie its reading to the reading of the regular will. In essence, this is your final gift of guidance and concern for your heirs, an "I'd like to say just one last time. . . ."

Such moments can mix some humor with the guidance. Opera diva Beverly Sills did not know that her father was dying (he kept the news from her). One night, on the way to a concert, she dropped by his hospital room.

"You look wonderful," her father said. "Don't let yourself get fat."

Beverly laughed. "Why do you think I'll let myself get fat?"

"Because you like ice cream too much."

Recalling that last conversation, Sills reminisces, "The truth of the matter is that I have always liked ice cream a lot. And as crazy as it sounds, I never take a bite of ice cream without thinking of him. Never."[95]

The ethical will of Sam Levinson, a well-known comedian and philosopher in the sixties and seventies, has been a model for many.

> To America I owe a debt for the opportunity it gave me to be free and to be me.
>
> To my parents I owe America. They gave it to me and I leave it to you. Take good care of it.
>
> To the biblical tradition I owe the belief that man does not live by bread alone, nor does he live alone at all. This is the democratic tradition. Preserve it.
>
> I leave you not everything I never had, but everything I had in my lifetime: a good family, respect for learning, compassion for my fellow-man, and some four-letter words for all occasions: words like "help," "care," "feel," and "love."
>
> Finally, I leave you the years I should like to have lived so that I might possibly see whether your generation will bring more love and peace to the world than ours did. I only hope you will. I pray that you will.[96]

Will your children say, "My father always believed in me . . ." or "my mother was my loudest cheerleader"? This is your chance to state one final time, in writing, your belief in or affirmation of a loved one. Consider doing this on video so that your eyes, your voice may be preserved, too.

A thought for reflection

When Jacob had finished giving instructions to his sons, he drew his feet up into the bed, breathed his last and was gathered to his people.

—Genesis 49:33

An audit

Take some moments to think about those who will survive you. What gifts in their lives would you like to recognize or encourage? What affirmation would you like to bestow on them?

To _____ I wish for you _____

To _____ I wish for you _____

To _____ I wish for you _____

To _____ I wish for you _____

To _____ I wish for you _____

To _____ I wish for you _____

A prayer

Father, I will not get to share the future with those I love.
Help me to find the words—
and the courage—to express those words
to "bless" their futures without me.

Breath meditation

Breathe in: My help is in the name of the Lord,

Breathe out: the Maker of heaven and earth. (Ps 124:8)

Composing your goodbyes

A good death gives us time to compose and share our goodbyes. Put it in writing. Letter-writing is a lost art in American society. Do you want to transmit your goodbyes in last-minute conversations and telephone calls, in less than ideal situations and environments, when you can say goodbye in a format that can be read, reread, and treasured?

Some will not only treasure the letter, the note, the card but also your handwriting. Letters or notes do not have to be long or elegant. You can draft a "scribe" to take dictation. Or you can use a video camera so that the goodbye can be seen and heard.

It is one thing to be told you are loved, valued, appreciated. It is something else to read that affirmation in writing, in handwriting. It can be hard to express ourselves in person. Anticipating and experiencing the initial reaction of the listener can short-circuit the process, particularly when talking about death. You may have to say, "Hear me out" or "let me finish." Through writing, such visual impediments are eliminated.

Consider writing a goodbye to those who are too young to "hear" the words, something like a time capsule. Write notes for graduation day, or a son or granddaughter's wedding or first baby.

Maybe you've read what Major Sullivan Ballou, Second Rhode Island Volunteers, wrote to his wife Sarah on the eve of a Civil War battle.

> My dear Sarah—
>
> If I do not return, my dear Sarah, never forget how much I loved you. Know that when my last breath escaped me on the battlefield, it will be your name that I whisper. Forgive my many faults and the many pains that I have caused you. How thoughtless, how foolish I have sometimes been. But, oh Sarah, if the dead can come back to this earth and flit unseen around those they love, I shall always be with you on the brightest day and the darkest night . . . always. And when the soft breeze fans your cheek, it shall be my breath or the cool air stirs your throbbing temple, it shall be my spirit passing by.[97]

One week after composing these words, Ballou died at the First Battle of Bull Run. Your words could be found just as meaningful by future generations.

A thought for reflection

Goodbye is the inevitable consequence of saying hello.

An audit

Something you write could stand the test of time. You begin with the first word of the first sentence of the first paragraph. Identify individuals to whom you would like to write goodbye.

To _____ saying _____

_____

To _____ saying _____

_____

To _____ saying _____

_____

To _____ saying _____

_____

To _____ saying _____

_____

A prayer

Jesus, how do I compose goodbye words
  when I do not want to say "Goodbye"?
Give me courage to find the words
  and to find ways to express the words
  to those I love,
  in ways they can best be heard.
  And re-heard.
Knowing that someday
  I will say "Hello" again
  in the land where goodbyes are unknown.

Breath meditation

Breathe in: I have suffered much;

Breathe out: preserve my life, O Lord. (Ps 119:107)

Food for the journey

People who know they are going to die spend their remaining time either being alive or staying alive.
—*Ted Menton*[98]

One way God comes to us and aids our dying is through *Viaticum*—the "food for the passage through death to eternal life." This gift reminds the baptized dying of the promise of God: "Those who eat my flesh and drink my blood have eternal life, and I will raise them up on the last day."

Whenever possible the dying Catholic should receive communion within Mass because of the public witness. However, contingencies may make that unlikely or impossible. It is important to renew your baptismal profession of faith. By doing so, you acknowledge who God is, and who you are—an individual needing God and the community of faith now more than ever before.

One of the most sobering moments on that tragic November day in 1963 was the announcement that a priest had administered "last rites" to President John F. Kennedy. That gift signaled that the wounds were substantial. No Catholic wanted to die without receiving last rites.

Unfortunately, as Mary Gordon points out, prior to the reforms of Vatican II, the narratives "always centered on the priest, arriving (like a Mountie on a horse) in the nick of time. The dying one was always more or less faceless and anonymous, unless he . . . was a great, very great sinner"[99] or a well-known politician. In essence, this individual's eternal life depended on a priest showing up in time. If Father arrived too late, there was "conditional absolution," but that was not as comforting to the loved ones.

The Rite of Anointing of the Sick has instituted several changes.

The focus is on the dying person. In fact, when the Anointing of the Sick is part of a mass, it gives recognition to the ill among us and creates an opportunity for parishioners to embrace them as part of the community. The dying are not the "lone rangers" but beloved children of God and part of a faith community.

Gordon insists that the sick, or dying, "having been anointed, are still the suffering, but they are not the afflicted."[100] Rather than keeping the ill out of sight (and out of mind), we honor them with sacred oil and rich symbolism. Who can forget the power of these words:

> Father in heaven, through this holy anointing, grant N. comfort in her suffering. When she is afraid, give her courage, when afflicted give her patience, when dejected afford her hope, and when alone, assure her of the support of your holy people.[101]

This prayer "names" the elements of spiritual suffering experienced by the dying (afraid, afflicted, dejected, alone). The church has not forgotten the example of Jesus' three friends, failing him in his dying.

The dying person is an active participant. Many times, too many times, the candidate for Extreme Unction was unaware of what was going on. The Anointing of the Sick will be more fully experienced and remembered by an active participant.

The dying are part of a long tradition. Others have, over the centuries, endured similar hardships in dying. The Apostle Paul underscores the reality, that "Since we are surrounded by such a great cloud of witnesses. . . let us run with perseverance the race marked out for us" (Heb 12:1). From the galleries of heaven, the saints cheer us on. As they were comforted in their hour of dying, now they become part of the "great cloud of witnesses" cheering us. They are experiencing the ultimate compassion of God, and now they witness you en route to receiving it!

"You are not alone in this." Jesus has never forgotten the sense of aloneness, abandonment he felt in his last hours. His groan "why have you forsaken me?" could easily have been directed to his friends Peter, James, and John. Still, Luke's gospel demonstrates that Jesus received "provision for the journey" when "an angel from heaven appeared to him and strengthened him" (22:43). The angel, however, did not appear to the disciples; you have to be awake to witness the extraordinary.

Mary Gordon writes,

> The sacrament of Anointing touches that part of the broken body that doctors, social workers, and loving family and friends cannot approach: the part that, in order to be healed, must acknowledge its despair and travel to a place of hope. And

that is what a sacrament must be: a vehicle for the
journey between the seen and the unseen.[102]

Perhaps, just before you've gone on a trip someone has said,
"Here, you'll need this." You may have responded, "What is it?"
and heard, "Oh, just something for your trip." *Viaticum* is "something" for the ultimate trip.

Someone may witness you receiving *viaticum* and think, "Oh,
yes, eucharist." But to you it is more—the promised provision for
the journey by a gracious God.

I live in Kansas City and am often reminded of the trails (the
Overland, the Oregon, and the Santa Fe) the pioneers followed to
their dreams in the West. I lead Grief Gatherings in Westport
where many brave souls bought their final provisions for the long
trek westward. The wise made certain of their provisions for this
journey.

The wise take up God's offered provisions for this ultimate
journey. It is only through the valley of the shadow that we make
our way into God's promised kingdom. I often close e-mail, "May
God give you strength sufficient for the demands of this day." God
offers that for the dying through the Anointing of the Sick.

A thought for reflection

The sacrament should be described as the sacred food which
strengthens the Christian for the passage through death to life in
sure hope of the resurrection.

—*Pastoral Care for the Sick*[103]

A prayer

Father, Outfitter,
   comfort me on this journey.
Whenever I am afraid, give me sufficient courage.
Whenever I am afflicted, give me sufficient patience.
Whenever I feel dejected, give me fresh hope.
Whenever I am alone, or feel alone,
   assure me of your love and presence.

Breath meditation

Breathe in: Jesus protect me

Breathe out: and lead me to eternal life!

Requesting and receiving the gifts of prayer

Pray for the strength to accept whatever comes your way—even if it is not what you asked for.
—*Harold Kushner[104]*

Before I would leave the hospital, I asked my father, "Anything I can do for you?" He always said, "Pray for me." One Christmas Eve, as I sat reading in his hospital room, thinking he was asleep, he snapped, "I wish you would do something for me."

"Sure, Dad. What do you need?" thinking that he wanted me to get him some water, call for a nurse, or change the channel on the television.

"I wish you would just take me out to the cemetery and leave me! I am no good for anyone any longer!" I dropped my book and climbed onto the bed. I took my dad's bony hand in mine and looked into his eyes. How many times, when I was a boy, had he comforted me? Now it was my turn to comfort.

"Dad, why do you say that? I could never do that!"

"I'm no good for anybody anymore." Certainly, my father was aware that his hospitalization was changing family members' plans for the holidays. The family was only gathering because he had insisted that it go on without him—a rehearsal for future Christmases.

You may find it difficult to ask for prayer. With some you need to offer guidance how you want them to pray. Alone, without someone to overrule, you may say, "That God will take me home to be with him." In the presence of certain family members, you may modify the request, "That I get well" or "get better."

Admittedly, you're supposed to pray, "Thy will be done, on earth as it is in heaven." But God's will is, well, difficult. Here are some other possibilities:

- Pray that I will be brave.
- Pray that I will be strong.
- Pray that I will remember the example of Jesus' dying.
- Pray that God will be close to me.
- Pray that I will be wise in making decisions.
- Pray that I will not be so afraid.
- Pray that my spouse or partner "deal" with the consequences.
- Pray for a son or daughter who is having a particularly difficult time.
- Pray for the nurses, orderlies, physicians caring for me.
- Pray for the grandchildren who are too young to understand.

Something happens when, as my friend Father Joe Nassal says, we "meet" in prayer, whether we're fifteen or fifteen hundred miles apart.

Give family and friends something to do: ask them to pray for you and pray *with* you.

A thought for reflection

. . .God wants our prayers and the prayers God wants are our prayers.

—Stanley Hauerwas[105]

A prayer

God, give me the courage to ask boldly!

Breath meditation

Breathe in: My comfort in my suffering is this:

Breathe out: Your promise preserves my life.
                  (Ps 119:50)

Embracing the silences

*In the silence of the heart God speaks. If you face God in prayer
and silence, God will speak to you.*
—Mother Teresa[106]

Some friends will be hesitant to talk to you; some are afraid of
saying the wrong thing, others are afraid of saying something
insensitive.

Of the children's books I use with grief groups, one favorite is
Arnold Lobel's *Alone*. Toad went to visit his friend Frog, but Frog
was not home and had left a note that he wanted to be alone. This
request puzzled Toad. "He has me for a friend. Why would he want
to be alone?" Toad searched until he found Frog sitting on an
island.

"Poor Frog!" Toad decided that a picnic lunch would cheer
up his friend. However, while crossing to the island, he fell
into the river. Now the pitcher of ice tea was empty and the

sandwiches were soggy. Toad had gone to this trouble so that Frog wouldn't be sad.

Frog explained that he wasn't sad but was happy. Happy because the sun was shining, happy because he was a frog, and happy because he had such a good friend. Frog wanted time alone to ponder all his blessings.

"So, the two stayed on the island all afternoon. They ate wet sandwiches, without the ice tea." Lobel concludes the tale, "They were two close friends sitting alone together."[107]

Blessed are you if you have friends with whom you can "sit alone together."

There will be times when you will be glad to be alone. Maybe there is just so much on your mind you need time to think. Make time to be alone on the deck, or in front of a fireplace, or in a favorite room in your home.

You may be dying but, like Frog, there is a lot of "fine" in your life, too.

Sometimes when there is nothing "more" to be said, a shared silence with a child, or spouse, or partner, or friend, or even a stranger can become a treasured gift.

Just as we need time to think, sometimes we need silence. Befriend the silence.

A thought for reflection

Sometimes God will wake us in the night to watch with Him and see things from a new perspective. Sometimes, it's the only time He can be sure of getting our complete attention. Sometimes that is the time, the exact time, when our prayers are needed.

—Celtic Daily Prayer[108]

A prayer

Stay with me, dear God, in the silences.
Bring me comfort so that those who gather with me
may find comfort in our silences.

Breath meditation

Breathe in: For this is our God;

Breathe out: he will be our guide even to the end.
                     (Ps 48:14)

Accepting the mystery

*Eternity will have to last a long time—I have enough questions
to fill up a thousand years.*
—Doug Manning[109]

Death does not always make sense. While humans can explore
the intricacies of the atom, or the farthest reaches of space, many
think death should also surrender its secrets.

Death can be like a giant jigsaw puzzle—uncompletable
because one or two of the pieces are missing.

You have choices—to grapple with the mystery or to be mad
as hell or as passive as a snail, mumbling, "Whatever."

Location, location, location is one governing principle in real
estate. Timing, timing, timing is one of the factors in trying to put
the experience of dying, particularly a premature death, into
perspective.

In this culture people want answers. Now. Individuals make good money as consultants supplying answers or what passes for answers or solutions. Death, however, is like a cagey poker player keeping his hand close to his chest.

Actually, the only functional question for you is, in all probability, *"Now what?"*

The Hawaiians have a word for this process of dancing with the mystery: *humuhumu*, which means fitting the pieces together.

In the 1600s, Jeremy Taylor observed, "A religion without mystery must be a religion without God."[110] Taylor's observation is still true. Southerners often sing out their theological questions. One favorite of mine reminds questioners, "We will understand it better, bye and bye."

You may have lots of questions; there will, unfortunately, be lots of "I don't know the answer to that." Seek out someone to whom you can verbalize your wonderings—someone who will listen all the way to the end of your sentences. Someone who will not offer simplistic answers.

Ironically, in the prayer after anointing, nothing is said about giving insight but rather comfort, courage, patience, and hope and the assurance of the support of the community of faith.

Unfortunately, in the last few years, there has been an effort in some quarters to "blame" the dying person. If you hadn't smoked so much . . . if you had taken better care of your health . . . if you hadn't had risky sex . . . if you had followed the doctor's orders . . . if you had positive attitudes. . . .

How is it possible that the heavy smoker avoids lung cancer; the individual who has never smoked does not? It's a mystery.

How is it possible that when two people received the same diagnosis, are treated by the same specialist, take the same pharmaceuticals, and are treated in the same medical center, one dies, one lives? It's a mystery.

Some would counsel that "Why me?" questions are pointless. Others suggest the answer is: "Why not me? Why should I be immune from suffering?"

Life is a mystery. Death is part of that mystery. Besides, answers rarely alter the prognosis.

Do not be in any hurry to solve the mystery.

A thought for reflection

When we accept that life is a mystery to be entered into,
we are able to be grateful for the gift of our lives—
even when we cannot make sense of all that happens.
—Wilkie Au[111]

An audit

Take a moment to think about your questions. What are the mysteries that wander the corridors of your heart and mind?

I wonder why_____

I wonder if_____

I wonder how_____

I wonder when_____

A prayer

God, the floors of my heart are littered with questions.
Remind me that you understand my questions
   and my questioning.
Give me grace to live with the mysteries.

Breath meditation

Breathe in: Come to me, all you who are weary . . .

Breathe out: and I will give you rest. (Mt 11:28)

Telling your stories

. . . the story of any one of us is in some measure the story of us all.
—Frederick Buechner[112]

You have a story to be told and a story that needs to be heard and honored. Unfortunately, a lot of people carry their stories to the grave with them. Whole chunks of a life can go untold, unknown, even by those who love you most.

You may be discounting your own story. "Who would be interested in my stories? Who needs the stories of another dying person?" In Chaim Potak's book *Old Men at Midnight*, the character Ilana answers, "I need them. Without stories there is nothing. Stories are the world's memory. The past is erased without stories."[113]

In too many families critical elements in family narratives disappear because they go untold, unheard. Sometimes family get only the skinniest version because there is no one to supply more details. Too commonly descendants learn the incredible stories only after the death of the loved one.

Weeks after my father's death, I received a letter from my father's oldest sister. She described a childhood incident in which she and my father were playing in the barn and were buried when a hay mound collapsed. Only the persistent barking of their dog alerted my grandfather and the men who rescued them. I would not be in this world had that dog not kept barking. So, why did my father never "remember" that story and pass it on?

You may decide you want to skip a generation and pass stories to grandchildren or great-grandchildren. One story may initiate questions that lead to more stories. "Well, now that you ask. . . ."

Your stories could be your greatest legacy. David Kessler wrote,

> The stories we have are who we are and they are what survives our death. No matter what our religion or culture, our stories will be told when we die. The telling may be in the form of a eulogy, an obituary, or a monument. Whatever form it takes, the story will be told at least one last time.[114]

Kessler adds, "People facing life-challenging illnesses want to tell us who they are, what they did for a living, about their families, their hopes, their dreams, their regrets"[115] and they want to point out the peculiarities of their lifepath.

Through storytelling you *humuhumu* seemingly unrelated pieces of your life together. You, as well as your listeners, could experience an electric "Ah-ha!" moment. One comment could summon another story deep in your mind and heart.

Your stories deserve to be passed on because stories contain the DNA of the spirit. Months, years after your death, one of your story fragments could be a source of inspiration and empowerment to those you love.

A thought for reflection

Account making is the way we spontaneously seek opportunities to tell and retell the stories of our loss and in so doing, recruit social validation for the changed stories of our lives.

—Robert Neimeyer[116]

An audit

Take some time to think about your life. Are there stories that you need to pass on?

I want to tell the story about the time _____

I want to tell the story about how I _____

I want to tell the story about the time _____ and I _____

I want to tell the story about the first time I ever _____

A prayer

Father, there are stories
    I have never had the courage to tell.
Give me the courage to own my stories
    and to share them with those I love.

Breath meditation

Breathe in: May the favor of the Lord

Breathe out: rest upon us. (Ps 90:17)

Holding on for special red-letter days

If you don't expect to see spring, when fall comes and you are around and you get to see spring, you don't experience it as spring. You experience it as an incredible miracle. Death transforms our living in ways in this culture we don't understand. See death as sugar; death gives life the pizzaz that makes it sweet.
Bill Bartholome[117]

Hanging on to experience red-letter days such as anniversaries, birthdays, graduations, weddings, first communions, championship games, or seasons such as Christmas or March Madness have been important to dying individuals. So, what are you waiting for?

Admittedly, someone may hint that your time line is unrealistic. But who is to say a desire is unrealistic? Some have befuddled all the doctors and specialists by holding on.

To fall short of the goal makes the special day or occasion rather bittersweet moments for survivors. "I wish he could have lived long enough to . . ." or "If only she could have lived just a little while longer. . . ."

So voice your expectation. Let someone witness it and share the expectation. Whenever someone tries to get you to adjust your plans "downward," remind yourself: "What does he know!"

One friend had the most remarkable father-in-law. After the diagnosis my friend asked, "Well, Pop, anything special that you want?"

"I want a birthday party," he responded, " a big birthday party with all the family here." So, the word went out. And to Kansas City they came. What's a birthday without cake and candles? Grandchildren and great-grandchildren squeezed in around him for the big moment. He took in all their faces, took a deep breath, as kids called out, "Don't forget to make a wish!" and blew out all the candles. And died.

"Oh, those poor children!" some have gasped hearing my friend tell the story. "I hope you got them into therapy right away."

"What 'poor children'!" she demands. "Pop got his wish. He died in the presence of all the family on a happy occasion. How many people get that?"

Make your wish known. Ask if you need help orchestrating it or arranging details, but that makes the getting sweeter. Anticipate someone wringing their hands and second-guessing the idea, "I don't know if this is such a good idea. . . ." (Most families have a designated party pooper.) Your courage may create a legend that will be passed to future generations. Your boldness may encourage some timid person to be more adventuresome when she experiences tough moments.

In the Genesis story, Jacob had bought the lie told him by his other sons that Joseph had been killed by a beast; he had held the blood-stained coat of many colors. So devastating was the loss that Jacob "refused to be comforted" and declared "in mourning will I go down to the grave" (37:35).

Jacob believed that his life—or at the least the best years of his life—was over without the favored son. No doubt, this obsessive grief drove the other brothers crazy. Joseph dominated their lives while he was alive and he continued to dominate their lives. No great home-cooked meals anymore; no great family gatherings. All of them were spoiled by the old man's long-running grief.

In the great twist in God's storying, years later Jacob feasts in Egypt on the turf of the son he thought dead. Finally, the old man is ill, dying. Joseph comes with his two Egyptian-born sons. In the presence of his grandsons, Jacob "rallied his strength and sat up in bed" (48:2).

Jacob asked, "Who are these?" What joy must have dashed through the patriarch's heart as he touched his flesh, Ephriam and Manasseh. He experienced what he had never imagined possible. Jacob did not go down to his grave, after all, in mourning—but with great joy.

What are you not imagining? What do you want to see? To taste? To touch? To experience? Ask God for that opportunity. God went to a great deal of logistics to balance the years of mourning Jacob had experienced. Your request may seem easy compared to that.

Give God a chance to work in your life. Ask outrageously.

A thought for reflection

Today is never an unlikely day
for something good to happen.

An audit

Take some time and think about what you want to live to experience.

I would like to live to experience _____

I would like to live to experience _____

I would like to live to experience _____

I would like to live to experience _____

I would like to live to experience _____

I would like to live to experience _____

Now, share this wish list with God. Don't be surprised if God responds, "We can do that." God often gives what Cajuns call "a little extra."

A prayer

God, all life is a gift from your hand.
Don't let me waste a moment of it.

Breath meditation

Breathe in: If any of you lacks wisdom,

Breathe out: let him ask God. (Jas 1:5)

Making room for humor

I discovered that when I was laughing, I couldn't be depressed. I couldn't be anxious. I couldn't be scared. It was like taking a vacation in the midst of all the chaos.
—A. Stephen Pieters[118]

Laughter has enormous healing power. Norman Cousins, after being diagnosed with ankylosing spondylitis, and given a one-in-five-hundred chance of surviving, devised his own healing regime: megadoses of Vitamin C and humor, particularly _Candid Camera, Abbott and Costello, I Love Lucy, The Three Stooges,_ and _The Marx Brothers._ He discovered that ten minutes of belly laughing became an anesthetic, giving him two hours of pain-free sleep. Cousins survived, wrote a bestseller on his experience, _Anatomy of an Illness,_ and joined the faculty of a medical school.[119]

Humor has a way of intruding on the most tense intimate dying scene. Stephen Pieters, facing death, asked friends to send him jokes instead of letters and get-well cards. He began and ended each day watching a sitcom. He adds, "I think it is important to find something to laugh about every single day because every single day there is certainly something not to laugh about."[120]

Dying people often appreciate dark humor because it defuses tension. Cardinal Bernardin—always a stickler for schedule—was concerned because his surgery was late. So Monsignor Ken Velo volunteered to inquire about the delay. Moments later he returned, smiling.

"Don't worry, Cardinal, the doctor is on his way. He's running a little late. He was arrested on a DUI charge last night." Velo's joking "broke the ice" and the Cardinal was wheeled into the operating room laughing.[121]

Sometimes, things "just happen" that are funny or strike us as funny. Allen Klein labels himself a *jollytologist*, a career he developed after the death of his wife from a rare liver disease. He not only makes people laugh, Klein teaches people how to laugh; he gives people permission to laugh. Klein finds humor in dying, as well as living—two sides of the same coin.

Klein's father-in-law, Jimmy, critically ill, was released from the hospital in time to celebrate his wedding anniversary at home. Klein urged him to invite some friends over, and he would cook. During the meal, Klein's mother-in-law noticed that her husband was tiring. Since he could not hear well, she wrote a note for Allen to pass to her husband. Allen read the note and burst out laughing. "What is so funny?" his father-in-law demanded.

Allen passed the note to Jimmy who read to the guests around the table: "Happy Anniversary, dear. Do you want to go to bed?" With a twinkle in his eye, and a smile, he replied, "I would love to, dear, but we have company."

After sharing the incident at Jimmy's memorial service, Klein concluded, "the laughter helped balance the pain and provided us with fond memories of his final hours."[122]

You may not have time to launch a career, but you could become a darn good amateur "jollytologist." You could end up being a stitch. Not to joke instead of confronting your prognosis, but to joke *in spite of* the prognosis.

As Cardinal John O'Connor was dying, Monsignor Gregory Mustaciuolo walked in to the Cardinal's office and cheerfully greeted him. "Good morning, Your Eminence. How do you feel?" The Cardinal looked up and asked, "About what?" (The Cardinal was known as a man of strong opinions!) Both Mustaciuolo and administrative assistant, Mary Ward, burst into laughter. She adds, "It was so characteristic of him, no matter what was going on, regardless of how sick he was, to find humor."[123]

You may not have to go looking for humor—it will find you. But, sometimes, you need a joke cued-up in your memory as a jump-starter.

Do not let any diagnosis rob you of your ability to laugh. Have you heard about the patient who after receiving the diagnosis, demanded a second opinion? "Okay," the doctor said, looking into his face, "You're ugly, too."

A thought for reflection

I started a one-woman adjustment crusade. Humor was my weapon of choice. I fought fearlessly against pessimistic self talk, and I killed all the depressing thoughts in my mind.

—Jinny Richerson[124]

An audit

If you could summons five comedians to do a free "command performance" for you and selected friends, who would you choose?

I would choose _____

I would choose _____

I would choose _____

I would choose _____

I would choose _____

A prayer

God, there's nothing funny about dying
  but there sure are plenty of funny things about living!
Help me to be humor-receptive today.
Ambush me with a belly laugh. I dare you.

Breath meditation

Breathe in: I will sing of the Lord's great love

Breathe out: forever. (Ps 89:1)

Part Three

Clinging to hope

Hope does not mean dreaming on about the future. Hope means aiming at it and just refusing to believe that you cannot make it.
—Maurice Lamm[125]

At the risk of sounding contradictory, hang on to your hope. Don't let anyone take your hope from you. Hope is a treasured companion. David Kessler, who has been there for many people, some famous like Michael Landon, tells a story about Sara. When she asked about an "alternative therapy," her physician snapped, "Sara, face it. There is no more hope." Sara responded without hesitation, "My hope is mine. I've had it all my life. Sometimes it becomes reality, sometimes it's just hope. I plan to keep my hope. In fact, I plan to die with it."[126]

You have a right to expect family, friends, and medical personnel to respect the boundaries of your hope.

A thought for reflection

You are always entitled to hold on to hope.
        —Harold Kushner[127]

A prayer

Jesus, you turned water into wine.
Great, unbelievable "save the best 'til last" wine.
Could you turn my grapes of doubt into hope?
Hope that will be sufficient for the demands of any day.
Nurture my frail seedlings of hope.

Breath meditation

Breathe in: Everyone who believes in the Son

Breathe out: has eternal life. (Jn 6:40)

Enjoying dessert

Life is short. Eat dessert first.
A bumper sticker

Think about all the people who skipped dessert that last night on *Titanic*. People are still skipping "desserts." How many times has life wanted to bring a tray of "desserts" to your table but you have waved it away?

So, what have you skipped? Maybe you have been so busy building a career or climbing the ladder to success that you haven't had a life. Have you been so busy being the "make it happen" person that you have not pampered yourself? That you haven't tasted life?

Desserts are not just sweets. Desserts are those moments spent watching a sunset, savoring a beach or a mountain vista, walking along a wooded path. Days spent leisurely soaking up the world around us.

John Loring's memory of his last lunch with Jackie Onassis is shaped by dessert. Whenever they ate at the trendy le Cirque in New York, the owner sent a sampling of desserts to their table. Jackie might stick her fork in and eat two crumbs (two crumbs!) and say, "Isn't that wonderful?" No "good to the last bite" for her. No running a fork around the plate like a vacuum cleaner.

That day, as the waiter placed four or five large desserts in front of them, Jackie startled Loring by saying: "You start that one. I'm going to eat this one."

"You're not going to finish that, are you? I'm going to have the waiter take this away right this moment," he said to her.

Mrs. Onassis interrupted him, "If anyone tries to touch one of these, I'm going to stab them in the hand with my fork. I'm going to eat every single one of them."

"And she did. We sat there and plowed through every single dessert on the table. It was astonishing. . . ."[128]

Maybe you've gone through life saying, "Just a small slice for me." Or "just enough to say I've had some" as one friend responds to dessert "opportunities."

What desserts have you skipped? Maybe it wasn't some caloric wonder that would have made Martha Stewart drool, but maybe some "lollygagging" moments when your "to do" list ruled! You may want to revisit some wasted moments.

Tom loved praline ice cream; so much that he arranged for it to be served at the end of his memorial service. Save some room for dessert.

An audit

Think about the five best desserts you have ever had. They were

_____

_____

_____

_____

_____

A prayer

God, in a culture that is so future-focused,
help me focus on "the desserts" my now offers.
I borrow words so many others have used.
I am confident that as you heard them
you will hear me:
"Into your hands I commend my spirit."

Breath meditation

Breathe in: Into your hands, Father,

Breathe out: I commit my spirit. (Ps 31:5a)

Choosing the time to die

Often the person dying will wait until he is alone in order to die. He had a reason. It's not to punish or to impose guilt, but rather the dying person desires privacy and solitude. This withdrawal offers the occasion to focus on the other world rather than to be pulled back into the realm of the living.
—Megory Anderson[129]

Is there a "right" time to die? You may decide to take death's hand while family members are away from the room or have fallen asleep. Or you may choose to wait until all of your family is present.

Virginia Morris shares a story about her grandma's habit of watching the Army-Navy football game. Her grandmother was not a sports fan, but she and her husband, a Navy veteran, had always watched the game together when he was alive. Her grandmother believed that "somehow" he was still watching it. "It was as close as she could get to him . . . it was her little romantic rendezvous."

After being ill only a few days her grandmother died. Morris pondered the timing. "She took her last breath hours before the start of the Army-Navy game. There was no doubt about her timing. Finally, Grandma was going to watch the Big Game with her man."[130]

There may come the moment when you ask your loved ones and friends to let you go.

A thought for reflection

My wife prays that God will help me to spend my last days living, rather than dying. I pray the same for others.

—Ed Dobson[131]

An audit

Take a moment and think about your family and friends and answer the following questions.

Who will have the most difficult time? _____

Who will be most resistant to letting you go? _____

Who will find your death too hard to witness? _____

_____

Whose permission do you need to die? _____

_____

A prayer

Father, letting go is more difficult than I imagined.
Only you know the moment you will say, "Come."
Give me the courage to live confidently in the meantime.

Breath meditation

Breathe in: Though I walk in the shadow of death

Breathe out: I will fear no evil. (Ps 23:4)

Finishing the race

One person's voice deserves to be heard above all others—yours. You have more at stake than anyone. So this is not a time to try to please everyone or to live up to others' expectations. It's a time to be true, above all, to yourself. It's a time to take control of your own decision making as much as you're able.
                                                    —James Miller[132]

The "very" end is always hard to figure out. People seem to have their own agendas about when the last breath will come. An acquaintance of mine was dying at home. Bills were paid, good-byes were said. About 1:00 a.m. he let out a scream that brought everyone running. "What?"

"I didn't," he gasped, "pay the American Express bill this month."

"What?" they groaned.

"I didn't pay the American Express bill!" he repeated. "I have to pay that bill. I've got to get my checkbook." He tried to get out of bed, but someone stopped him. Again, he stated his determination to pay that bill. Finally, someone found the bill and the checkbook, and Larry scribbled out the check. "Anything else?" someone inquired.

An hour later Larry died, thankfully with the American Express bill paid. God forbid that he had died with an unpaid balance! I think about him often—when I pay my American Express bill.

Some simply slip away. Some die in their sleep. Some stir for just a moment and offer an invitation to someone to calm them or hold their hand.

As Robert Veninga walked toward his office one frigid Minnesota morning, he happened to look up into a window at the Masonic Cancer Center at the University of Minnesota. A sign, apparently written by a patient, read, "I need a large sausage pizza!"

Veninga smiled at such resourcefulness. "Here was a patient, possibly living out his last days of life, who had retained a sense of humor and knew how to ask for what he wanted."

Throughout the day, Dr. Veninga's mind darted back to that sign. Finally, he telephoned the nurses' station to ask if they were aware of the sign.

"Oh yes. You ought to meet that patient. He has one of the most virulent forms of cancer, but his spirit is amazing. He just won't give up!"

"Did anyone bring him a pizza?"

"By noon his room was lined from door to the window with large sausage pizzas. We had enough pizza to feed everyone in the unit."[133]

A patient asked. He received. His voice was heard.

God knows your death moment. God promises to be with you in that last breath. And, apparently, sometimes, God comes disguised as a pizza delivery man. When God says "never" in "Never will I leave you; never will I forsake you" (Heb 13:5), he means *never*!

A thought for reflection

The word goodbye—originally "God-be-with-ye" or "Go-with-God"—was a recognition that God was a significant part of the going.

—Joyce Rupp[134]

A prayer

God, it is becoming apparent that I am not going to get
the miracle that I, and others, have prayed for.
In the moments when my confidence wanes,
when my trust falters,
remind me of your promise to accompany me,
safely toward and into this new arena of my life:
Eternity!

Breath meditation

Breathe in: Never will God leave me

Breathe out: or abandon me. Never!

Endnotes

1. Saint Anthony the Great in Ronda DeSola Chervin (Ed.). (1992). *Quotable Saints*. Ann Arbor, MI: Charis/Servant Books, 74.
2. Kenneth Vaux & Sara Vaux. (1996). *Dying Well*. Nashville, TN: Abingdon, 11.
3. Joseph Bernardin. (1997). *The Gift of Peace: Personal Reflections by Joseph Cardinal Bernardin*. Chicago: Loyola University Press, 3.
4. *Ibid.*, 59.
5. Venerable Charles de Foucauld in *Quotable Saints*, 183.
6. Megory Anderson. (2001). *Sacred Dying: Creating Rituals for Embracing the End of Life*. Roseville, CA: Prima Publishing, 114.

7. Donna Schaper. (1991). *Stripping Down: The Art of Spiritual Restoration.* San Diego, CA: Luramedia, 47.

8. Virginia Morris. (2001). *Talking About Death Won't Kill You.* New York: Workman, 67.

9. Patti LaBelle. (2001). *Patti's Pearls: Lessons in Living Genuinely, Joyfully, Generously.* New York: Warner Books, 53.

10. Henri Nouwen. (1993). *Our Greatest Gift: A Meditation on Dying and Caring.* San Francisco: HarperSanFrancisco, 109.

11. Andre Lorde. (2001). In Studs Terkel, *Will the Circle Be Unbroken?* New York: New Press, 320.

12. Len Butler. (1999, 6 June). Testimony. Knoxville, TN: Central Baptist Church of Bearden.

13. David Wolpe. (1999). *Making Loss Matter: Creating Meaning in Difficult Times.* New York: Riverhead Books, 5.

14. Jimmy Carter & Rosalynn Carter. (1987). *Everything to Gain: Making the Most of the Rest of Your Life.* New York: Random House, 7.

15. St. John Bosco in *Quotable Saints*, 151.

16. Dave Dravecky, Jan Dravecky, with Ken Gire. (1992). *When You Can't Come Back: A Story of Courage and Grace.* Grand Rapids, MI: Zondervan, 144.

17. Frederica Mathewes-Green. (1999). *At the Corner of East and Now: A Modern Life in Ancient Christian Orthodoxy*. New York: Jeremy T. Tarcher, 57.

18. Rainer Maria Rilke. (2001). *Letters to a Young Poet*. New York: Modern Library, 34-35.

19. Hamilton Jordan. (2000). *No Such Thing as a Bad Day: A Memoir by Hamilton Jordan*. New York: Pocket Books, 143.

20. John Eagan. (1990). *Traveler Toward Dawn: The Spiritual Journal of John Eagan, S.J.* William J. O'Malley (Ed.). Chicago, IL: Loyola University Press, 152.

21. Jordan, 213.

22. Morris, 75.

23. Leo Rosten. (1977). *Leo Rosten's Treasury of Jewish Quotations*. New York: Bantam, 449.

24. Morrie Schwartz. (1996). *Letting Go: Morrie's Reflections on Living While Dying*. New York: Walker and Company, 30.

25. Barbara Bush. (1994). *Barbara Bush: A Memoir*. New York: Charles Scribner's Sons, 44.

26. Mitch Albom. (1997). *Tuesdays with Morrie: An Old Man, A Young Man, and Life's Greatest Lesson*. New York: Doubleday, 151.

27. Kenneth Velo. (1996, 20 November). *Homily at Funeral Mass of His Eminence Joseph Cardinal Bernardin*, 7.

28. Parker Palmer. (2001, 31 October). Lecture, Metropolitan Community College, Kansas City, MO.
29. Matta Kelley in Terkel, 310.
30. *Ibid.*, 311.
31. Morris, 234.
32. Linda Johnson, Midwest Bioethics Center. Personal correspondence.
33. Jordan, 236.
34. *Ibid.*
35. Morris, 244-245.
36. Jordan, 231.
37. David Kessler. (1997). *The Rights of the Dying: A Companion for Life's Final Moments.* New York: HarperCollins, 47.
38. *Ibid.*, 52.
39. *Ibid.*, 160.
40. Been There in Chicago. (1994, 6 July). Letter to Ann Landers. *The Kansas City Star*, F-6.
41. Northumbria Community. (2000). *Celtic Daily Prayer.* London: HarperCollins Religious, 224.
42. Mark Twain, cable to Associated Press from London, 1897 in Emily Morrison Beck (Ed.). (1980). *Familiar Quotations by Bartlett* (15th ed.). Boston: Little, Brown, 625.
43. Jim Mohr. (2001, 23 September). "When the game is on the line, go to Bingham." *The San Francisco Examiner.*

44. International Commission on English in the Liturgy. (1983). *Pastoral Care of the Sick: Rites of Anointing and Viaticum*. New York: Catholic Book Publishing Company, 112.

45. Quinn Brisben in Terkel, 216.

46. Edward Klein. (1998). *Just Jackie: Her Private Years*. New York: Ballantine, 359-360.

47. Anderson, 149.

48. Eagan, 150.

49. Rowan Williams in *Celtic Daily Prayer*, 48.

50. John Hewett. (1980). *After Suicide*. Wayne E. Oates (Ed.). Louisville, KY: Westminister Press, 48.

51. Kathleen Fischer. (1998). Hannah Ward and Jennifer Ward (Compilers). *The Doubleday Christian Quotation Collection*. New York: Doubleday, 262.

52. *Celtic Daily Prayer*, 722.

53. Bernardin, 39.

54. Stephen E. Ambrose. (1991). *Nixon: Ruin and Recovery, 1973-1990*. New York: Simon & Schuster, 514-515.

55. John Paul II. (1994). *The Private Prayers of John Paul II: Words of Inspiration*. New York: Pocket Books, 133.

56. Margaret Hebblethwaite in *Doubleday*, 272.

57. Mick Betancourt in Terkel, 345.

58. Will D. Campbell. (1986). *Brother to a Dragonfly*. New York: Continuum, 220.

59. Eagan, 151.
60. Harold Kushner. (2001, 26 April.) "Conversations at the End of Life: Sharing Sacred Stories." Midwest Bioethics Lecture, Kansas City, Missouri.
61. Michael Evlanoff and Marjorie Fluor. (1969). *Alfred Nobel: The Loneliest Millionaire.* Ward Ritchie Press.
62. Meg McSherry Breslin. (1998, 22 March). "Moods of Funerals Changing." *The Chicago Tribune*, Section 4, 2-3.
63. Larry McMurtry. (1995). *The Late Child.* New York: Simon and Schuster, 267.
64. Mary Oliver. (1991). "When Death Comes," in *New and Selected Poems.* Boston: Beacon Press, 10-11.
65. *http://www.chebucto.ns.ca/Philosophy/Sui-Generis/Emerson/success.htm.*
66. Obituary: Florence McNaul Muller. (2001, 28 October). *The Kansas City Star*, B6.
67. Adapted from Liturgy of Reconciliation.
68. Keith Caraway in Tim Hansel. (1986). *You Gotta Keep Dancin'.* Elgin, IL: David C. Cook, 143.
69. Bernie Siegel. (1986). Lecture, Temple B'nai Jehudah. Kansas City, Missouri.
70. Eleanor Roosevelt. (2001, 13 November). "Overheard." *The Kansas City Star*, E3.

71. Dag Hammarskjold. (1965). *Markings*. Translated by Leif Sjoberg and W. H. Auden. New York: Knopf, 89.

72. William Bartholome. (1999). "A Prayer." Kansas City, MO: Midwest Bioethics Center.

73. Mark Schel in Jill Dutton. (2001, 23 August). "An Attitude of Gratitude." *The Kansas City Star*, E3.

74. Ted Menton. (1991). *Gentle Closings: How to Say Goodbye to Someone You Love*. Philadelphia: Running Press, 58.

75. Pam Bartholome on Bill Moyers' PBS Special: "On Our Own Terms." (2000, 10 September).

76. Andy Morrison. (1995, 11 November). "Burger Left 'Inadequate' Will, and It Could Cost Heirs a Lot." *The Kansas City Star*, A-4.

77. *Ibid.*, 1.

78. *Ibid.*

79. Eleanor Roosevelt. Retrieved from www.senior-center.com/eleanor1.htm.

80. Beatrice Ash, with Lucille Allen. (1993). *A Time to Live, A Time to Die*. Minneapolis: Augsburg, 37.

81. *Ibid.*

82. *The Celtic Daily Prayer*, 476.

83. Joseph Lash. (1972). *Eleanor: The Years Alone*. New York: W. W. Norton, 329.

84. Klein, 363-364.

85. Matthew Fox in *Doubleday*, 263.

86. Dietrich Bonhoeffer. (1954). *Life Together.* Trans. by John W. Doberstein. New York: Harper & Row, 99.

87. Schwartz, 73.

88. Albom, 33.

89. Jerry Porter. (2001, August) "Commission: Saints Suffer Too." *Holiness Today*, 49.

90. Cornelius Ryan and Katheryn Morgan Ryan. (1974). *A Private Battle.* New York: Simon and Schuster, 354.

91. "A Trivia Expert, Some Music Lovers, Along with Expectant Fathers." (2001, 8 November). *The New York Times*, B12.

92. Kessler, 166.

93. Patricia Weenolsen. (1996). *The Art of Dying: How to Leave This World With Dignity & Grace, At Peace With Yourself & Your Loved Ones.* New York: St. Martin's, 56.

94. Kerry M. Olitzky & Ronald H. Isaacs. (1996). *The Second How-to Handbook for Jewish Living.* Hoboken, NJ: KTAV Publishing House, 88.

95. Beverly Sills & Larry Linderman. (1987). *Beverly:An Autobiography.* New York: Bantam, 45.

96. Sam Levinson. (1991). *So That Your Values Live On.* Jack Reimer (Ed.). Woodstock, VT: Jewish Lights,168.

97. Sullivan Ballou (1861, 14 July). *Brown University Alumni Quarterly* (1990 November), 38-42.

98. Ted Menton, *Gentle Closings*, 57.
99. Mary Gordon. (2000). In Thomas Grady & Paula Huston (Eds.). *Signature of Grace: Catholic Writers on the Sacraments*. New York: Dutton, 204.
100. *Ibid.*
101. *Pastoral Care of the Sick*, 112.
102. Gordon, 218.
103. *Pastoral Care of the Sick*, 163.
104. Kushner, 26 April 2001.
105. Stanley Hauerwas. (1999). *Prayers Plainly Spoken*. Downer's Grove, IL: InterVarsity Press, 17.
106. Mother Teresa in Alan Fensin. (1995). *Life: The Owner's Manual*. Metarie, LA: Way Enterprises, 81.
107. Lobel, Arnold. (1979). *Days with Frog and Toad*. New York: HarperCollins, 64.
108. *Celtic Daily Prayer*, 536.
109. Doug Manning. (1979). *Don't Take My Grief Away.* San Francisco, Harper & Row, 47.
110. Jeremy Taylor in *Doubleday*, 134.
111. Wilkie Au. (2000). *The Enduring Heart: Spirituality for the Long Haul*. New York: Paulist Press, 147.
112. Frederick Buechner. (1982). *The Sacred Journey*. New York: HarperCollins, 6.

113. Curt Schleier. (2001, 11 November). "Potok Weaves Seemingly Simple Stories, Rich in Context." [Book Review]. *The Kansas City Star*, J7.

114. Kessler, 5.

115. *Ibid.*

116. Robert A Neimeyer. (1998). *Lessons of Loss: A Guide to Coping*. New York: McGraw-Hill/Primis Custom Publishing, 94.

117. Bartholome, "On Our Own Terms."

118. A. Stephen Pieters. (1998). In Allen Klein. *The Courage to Laugh: Humor, Hope, and Healing in the Face of Death and Dying*. New York: Jeremy P. Tarcher/Putnam, 117.

119. Norman Cousins. (1979). *Anatomy of an Illness*. New York: W.W. Norton.

120. Pieters, 118.

121. Bernardin, 67.

122. Klein, 6.

123. Terry Golway. (2001). *Full of Grace: An Oral Biography of John Cardinal O'Connor*. New York: Pocket Books, 209.

124. Jinny Richerson. (2001, 2 December). In "Just Laugh." *The Kansas City Star*, G1, G6.

125. Maurice Lamm. (1969). *The Power of Hope*. New York: Jonathan David Publishers, 32.

126. Kessler, 11.

127. Kushner, 26 April 2001.

128. Klein, 359.

129. Anderson, 199.

130. Morris, 109-110.

131. Marshall Shelley, Eric Reed & Drew Zahn (Eds.). (2001, Fall). "Leave Room for God: Leadership Interview with Ed Dobson." *Leadership*, 34.

132. James Miller. (1997). *When You Know You're Dying: 12 Thoughts to Guide You Through the Days Ahead*. Ft. Wayne, IN: Willowgreen Publications, 29.

133. Robert Veninga. (1985). *A Gift of Hope: How We Survive Our Tragedies*. Boston: Little, Brown, 224-225.

134. Joyce Rupp. (1988). *Praying Our Goodbyes*. Notre Dame, IN: Ave Maria Press, 17.

Harold Ivan Smith is an adjunct professor in the doctoral program at Northern Baptist Seminary and has taught courses at Nazarene Theological Seminary. He is a public speaker who frequently leads workshops for hospice training events and pastoral leadership conferences. He is the author of many books on bereavement. He lives in Kansas City, Missouri.